Quick & Easy
One-Pot
Casseroles

Quick & Easy One-Pot Casseroles

Jean Conil

foulsham

LONDON • NEW YORK • TORONTO • SYDNEY

foulsham

The Publishing House
Bennetts Close, Cippenham, Berks SL1 5AP

ISBN 0-572-01982-3

Cover photograph © Food Features
Typeset in England by Typesetting Solutions, Slough, Berks.
Printed in England by Cox & Wyman Ltd, Reading, Berks.

CONTENTS

BACKGROUND

JEAN CONIL WAS TRAINED IN PARIS and inspired by Escoffier whom he met in 1932. He worked in the south of France and on board luxury French liners in pre-war days. He became well known for his articles on cookery in the *Sunday Times* and in magazines. He is the author of more than 100 cookery books including the best sellers: *French Home Cookery, Haute Cuisine* and *Cuisine Vegetarienne Française.*

Jean Conil was the Executive Chef and Catering Manager of Fortnum and Mason, The Hurlingham Club, the Arts Club and the Athenaeum Hotel in Park Lane. He is the Founder and Life Administrative President of the prestigious Epicurean World Master Chefs' Society.

NOTES ON THE RECIPES

- Ingredients are given in metric, Imperial and American measures. Use only one set per recipe, don't interchange.
- All spoon measures are level.
- Eggs are size 3 unless otherwise stated.
- All herbs are fresh unless otherwise stated. To substitute dried, use half the quantity as they are very pungent.
- Wash, dry and peel when necessary fresh produce before using.
- Preparation and cooking times given at the end of each recipe are approximate and should be used as a guide only.
- Make sure the casserole dish you use is the correct size to hold the ingredients comfortably. If it is over-full, it will take longer to cook. If the dish is too large the ingredients may dry out.
- For seasoned flour use 2.5 ml (½ tsp) salt and a good pinch of freshly ground black pepper to 50 g (2 oz) flour.

INTRODUCTION

THE WORD 'CASSEROLE' IS USED TO describe a lidded vessel in which the ingredients are cooked slowly, usually in the oven. By extension, the name *casserole* is also applied to the dishes cooked in such containers.

The wonderful thing about them is they are very quick to prepare and then can be left to cook gently with the minimum of attention so nothing could be easier.

The other great advantage is you can use inexpensive cuts of meat and still create tender and delicious dishes.

In this book, the same pot is used for the preparation, cooking and serving of the dish, so there's very little washing up too! Choose a casserole made of cast iron, stainless steel, copper, ceramic or earthenware with a heavy base which can be used on top of the cooker when ingredients need some pre-cooking and then in the oven. Look for the words *flameproof* and *ovenproof* on the label.

Many dishes in the book are meals in themselves, others would benefit from some crusty bread, a fresh vegetable, rice or a green salad. To save time and money, pop some jacket potatoes or a smaller casserole dish with some diced root vegetables in the oven at the same time.

NOTE: You could use an electric slow cooker for these recipes, but refer to your manual for cooking times.

CASSEROLED COUNTRY SOUPS

FOR CENTURIES PEASANT SOUPS WERE produced from a black pot-type of casserole suspended over the fire in farm households. These hot pot soups were covered with a lid and the contents – meat and vegetables – simmered gently for hours until the quintessence of the ingredients, enhanced by herbs, produced a wonderfully concentrated flavour with barely any effort at all. Such nectar soups were meals in themselves, being hot-pot cum stews cum casseroles. Of these ancient soups there are many which have stood the test of time.

Fortifying Soups

All soups can be fortified with meat or yeast extracts, or stock cubes dissolved in water. Extra garnishes, such as bread sippets, cooked rice or vermicelli that complement the ingredients can be added for extra sustenance. Country soups that use pulses and beans are extremely nourishing and provide a wholesome and varied diet. For a richer flavour, pan fry (sauté) the meat and vegetables first.

Catherine's Bortsch

A bortsch, by definition, is a soup made with beetroot, giblets, bacon and old duck pieces served with a garnish of soured cream. The dominating flavour of fennel enhances this soup, which was a favourite of that famous Russian, Catherine the Great.

∾ SERVES 4 ∾

4 legs of duck
4 rashers (slices) back bacon
1 raw beetroot (red beet), sliced
1 fennel bulb, sliced
neck and giblet of one duck
1.25 l (2¼ pts · 5½ cups) water
Salt and freshly ground black pepper

Garnish:
1 cooked beetroot (red beet), cut into strips
120 ml (4 fl oz · ½ cup) red wine
15 ml (1 tbsp) wine vinegar
150 ml (¼ pt · ⅔ cup) soured (dairy sour) cream

1. Place all the main ingredients in a metal casserole (Dutch oven) and cover with water. Cover and braise slowly in the oven for 2 hours at 180°C/350°F/gas mark 4.

2. In a sauce boat combine the beetroot strips, wine and vinegar. Either blend this into the soup at the last moment or serve it separately with a jug of soured cream.

The solid ingredients can be served with the liquid in individual soup bowls from the casserole. Alternatively, the liquid and garnish, and the duck and bacon may be served separately. The old-fashioned way is to serve all the ingredients together with wholemeal country bread.

Preparation time: 10 minutes.
Cooking time: 2 hours.

King Louis' Consommé

It is said that the French King Louis XVI over-ate too often and needed tonic broths to revive his appetite. His chef gave him one day such a concentrated beef-tea that the King felt it was the best medicine he had ever had.

───────────────── ∽ SERVES 4 ∽ ─────────────────

450 g (1 lb · 2 cups) lean minced (ground) beef
50 g (2 oz · ½ cup) beetroot (red beet), peeled and grated
25 g (1 oz · ¼ cup) onion, chopped
50 g (2 oz · ½ cup) carrots, grated
25 g (1 oz · ¼ cup) fennel, grated
1 egg white
Salt and freshly ground black pepper
1.2 l (2 pts · 5 cups) beef stock
150 ml (¼ pt · ⅔ cup) white port

1. Combine all the ingredients in a casserole (Dutch oven). Leave to soak for 1 hour.

2. Cover with a lid and braise in moderate oven for 2 hours at 180°C/350°F/gas mark 4. The solids will gradually come to the top and form a thick crust during cooking. The liquid will be clear, limpid and aromatic.

To serve the consommé, simply make a small hole in the crust, ensuring that the rest remains unbroken, and remove the liquor. Alternatively, you can strain the consommé through a muslin cloth (cheesecloth). The solids are discarded completely. This is the best way to produce a beef tea.

Preparation time: 10 minutes plus soaking time.
Cooking time: 2 hours.

Cassoulet Soup

This soup is made with goose or duck legs which are cooked in plenty of liquid with haricot beans and tomatoes until the meat is completely separated from the bones and the beans soft enough to be puréed or liquidised to make a thick soup.

─────────────── ∾ SERVES 4 ∾ ───────────────

2 duck or goose drumstick legs
30 ml (2 tbsp) oil or fat
100 g (4 oz · 1 cup) haricot (navy) beans, soaked in water overnight
1 onion, sliced
1 carrot, sliced
1 onion, chopped
2 garlic cloves, crushed
Salt and freshly ground black pepper
1.2 l (2 pts · 5 cups) water and wine in equal quantities

1. Put all the ingredients in a metal pot with a lid on top. Braise gently for 2 hours at 180°C/350°F/gas mark 4. Liquidise the soup to a thin purée and serve with French bread.

Preparation time: 5 minutes plus soaking time.
Cooking time: 2 hours.

Mathilda Soup

Delicious, tasty poultry soups can be produced in casseroles using only giblets, winglets, necks, and cleaned gizzards. This recipe has been in my family for years. The delicate aroma of leeks slightly enhances the natural flavour of chicken. Using the skin from the chicken gives the soup more flavour.

∽ SERVES 4 ∾

1 kg (2¼ lb) mixed giblets, (winglets, neck etc)
50 g (2 oz · ¼ cup) butter
2 leeks, sliced, washed, drained and dried
150 g (5 oz · 1¼ cups) potato, finely diced
Salt and freshly ground black pepper
1.2 l (2 pints · 5 cups) water
2 chicken stock cubes
Double (heavy) cream (optional)

1. Wash the giblets. Drain and dry. Place in a metal casserole (Dutch oven) and brown for 5 minutes in the butter. Add leeks and potato. Season to taste. Add water and stock cubes. Cover with a lid and cook slowly for 1½ hours at 180°C/350°F/gas mark 4.

For a richer soup, serve a sauce boat of double cream from which your guests can help themselves.

Preparation time: 10 minutes.
Cooking time: 1½ hours.

Thick Pea Soup

Split peas are at their best when cooked in casseroles where they make a thickish type of soup. Always popular, this well known English soup is made more interesting when cooked with unsmoked bacon.

To make crispy, fried bread croûtons, cut the crusts off some sliced bread and cut it into squares. Sprinkle liberally with olive oil, toss well, then bake in a preheated oven at 200°C/400°F/gas mark 6 for about 10 minutes, stirring occasionally until crisp and golden.

───────────── ∾ SERVES 4 ∾ ─────────────

150 g (5 oz · ⅓ cup) split peas, soaked in cold water for 2 hours
1 onion, chopped
1 celery stick, chopped
6 spinach leaves, shredded
150 g (5 oz · scant 1 cup) back bacon,
including fat but rinded and diced
1.25 l (2¼ pts · 5½ cups) water

Garnish:
150 g (5 oz · 1¼ cups) fried bread croûtons

1. Put all the main ingredients in a metal casserole (Dutch oven). Braise slowly for 1½ hours at 180°C/350°F/gas mark 4. Strain the soup or liquidise to a thin purée.

Serve the fried croûtons separately.

Preparation time: 10 minutes plus soaking time.
Cooking time: 1½ hours.

Canadian Cod Chowder

The word 'chowder' is an old word for the French *chaudron*, a cast iron casserole pot which fishermen use constantly for their meals. The inland equivalent of the chowder is probably beef *pot au feu*. The term chowder, however, is more usually applied to a casserole of fresh or salted cod. It can be tastier and simpler to prepare than a complicated bisque. The combination of fish and vegetables makes this a really healthy meal. This soup will have a more intense fish flavour if made with a fish stock.

———————————— ∾ SERVES 4 ∾ ————————————

50 g (2 oz · ¼ cup) butter
1 kg (2¼ lb) cod, skinned, boned, and cubed
1 onion, chopped
1 carrot, chopped
1 celery stick, chopped
5 ml (1 tsp) dried thyme
225 g (8 oz · 2 cups) potatoes, diced
3 basil leaves, chopped
1.25 l (2¼ pts · 5½ cups) water or fish stock
Salt and freshly ground black pepper

1. Layer the butter and all the other ingredients in a casserole (Dutch oven). Cover level with water. Season and cover with a lid. Braise slowly for 1 hour at 180°C/350°F/gas mark 4. When cooked, serve in warmed soup bowls.

Preparation time: 10 minutes.
Cooking time: 1 hour.

African Lamb Soup with Couscous

Lamb is extremely popular all over northern Africa and most countries in the region produce their own version of these types of soup cum casserole broths. It is the pungency of the herbs and spices such as fennel, saffron, cumin, garlic and chillies that give the couscous soup its distinctive and wholesome character.

―――――――――――― ∾ SERVES 6 ∾ ――――――――――――

225 g (8 oz · 2 cups) lean lamb from neck or shoulder, diced
1 fennel bulb, diced
1 carrot, diced
1 celery stick, sliced
1 courgette (zucchini), sliced
1 green chilli, sliced
1 onion, sliced
2 garlic cloves, chopped
Pinch of cumin seed
Pinch of ground saffron
1.25 l (2¼ pts · 5½ cups) water
Extra garnish:
50 g (2 oz · ⅓ cup) couscous
25 g (1 oz · 2 tbsp) butter

1. Put all the ingredients in a casserole (Dutch oven) and braise gently for 2 hours at 180°C/350°F/gas mark 4.

2. Ten minutes before serving, rub the couscous with melted butter and stir it into the hot soup. Cook for the remaining 10 minutes.

Preparation time: 15 minutes.
Cooking time: 2 hours.

King Henry Hot Pot Soup

Henry IV, King of Navarre and France, was the first monarch to take an interest in agriculture, recognising the need for more and better food for the impoverished French people. "I want everyone in France," he said, "to be able to afford a chicken once a week in the soup pot." At that time the diet of the ordinary workers was very meagre and largely vegetarian.

——————————— ∽ SERVES 6 ∽ ———————————

1 small oven-ready chicken (or other fowl)
2 leeks, sliced
2 carrots, sliced
1 turnip, diced
1 celery stick, diced
1 sprig of thyme
1.75 l (3 pts · 7½ cups) water
5 ml (1 tsp) salt
6 crushed peppercorns

1. Put all the ingredients in a casserole (Dutch oven), cover with a lid and gently cook at 180°C/350°F/gas mark 4 for 1¼ hours.

2. When done remove the chicken. Then, either carve it into portions and serve it with the vegetables and broth, or liquidise the vegetables in the stock for a thick soup and serve the chicken separately as a garnish or as a main course.

Preparation time: 5 minutes.
Cooking time: 1¼ hours.

Chapter Two

SEAFOOD CASSEROLES

THE GREAT CLASSICAL SEAFOOD dishes are often those baked in casseroles, and many of them suit this type of cooking very well. By using this method the most delicious fish dishes can be produced out of ordinary and very cheap fish.

Many rice and fish combinations are cooked in casseroles in 20–25 minutes. The flavour of large pieces of fish on the bone benefits from being baked with sliced potatoes. In this chapter I have selected the most tasty fish casseroles which are simple to prepare in next to no time and don't take as long as meat to cook either.

When buying fish, look for signs of quality: shining skin, pink gills, and full bright eyes with black pupils and transparent corneas. The flesh should be firm and springy. Fresh fish should have a clean, pleasant odour. (The exception to this rule is the ammoniac smell found in skate, the shark family, and rays.) Look for fish with translucent, rather than milky, flesh. Fillets that are dried up around the edges and show traces of discolouration will be stale.

If you buy fish whole, gut them as soon as possible as the digestive organs contain powerful enzymes that will attack the body wall. The only ones that can be kept intact for any length of time are fish like salmon and sea trout, because during the breeding season, when they are caught, the digestive organs of these fish waste away.

Sea food will not keep for more than a day or two in a fridge and should be loosely wrapped in cling film (plastic wrap) or foil to prevent the smell from spreading and contaminating other foods. All fish should be washed in salt water with a little vinegar (15 ml/1 tbsp per 600 ml/1 pint) before cooking.

Fresh fish is often dressed when purchased, that is gutted with scales and fins removed. To ensure the fish you buy is really fresh, ask to see the skin and the head of the fish before you purchase it.

Most fish benefit from being marinated or cooked in water or oils flavoured with herbs. A fresh herring or mackerel, however, requires nothing more than a knob of butter and a squeeze of lemon juice.

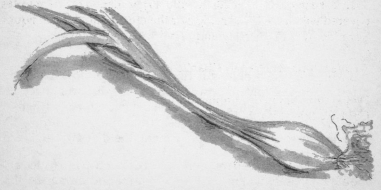

Cod Casserole with Cheese

The curry powder adds piquancy to the fish.

―――――――――――――――――― ∾ SERVES 4 ∾ ――――――――――――――――――

60 ml (4 tbsp) seasoned flour
5 ml (1 tsp) curry powder
1 kg (2¼ lb) skinned cod fillet cut into 4 or 6 portions
40 g (1½ oz · 3 tbsp) butter, melted
1 shallot, chopped
4 mushrooms, sliced
Salt and white pepper
75 ml (5 tbsp) dry white wine
Small sprig of thyme, chopped
75 ml (5 tbsp) hot water
1 fish stock cube dissolved in the hot water
45 ml (3 tbsp) Cheddar cheese, grated
60 ml (4 tbsp) double (heavy) cream
45 ml (3 tbsp) chopped parsley

1. Combine the seasoned flour with the curry powder and use to coat the cod fillets.

2. Pour the melted butter into a casserole dish (Dutch oven). Sprinkle the shallot and mushrooms over the butter and lay the fish fillets on top. Season to taste. Add wine, thyme and fish stock. Sprinkle over the grated cheese.

3. Bake in the oven at 200°C/400°F/gas mark 6 for 20 minutes, covered with a lid. On serving, stir the cream into the fish liquor. Sprinkle over the parsley and serve with crusty bread.

 Ideal with Muscadet, Chablis or dry cider.

Preparation time: 10 minutes.
Cooking time: 20 minutes.

Tuna Provençale

In an emergency you could use canned tuna.

─────────── ∾ SERVES 6 ∾ ───────────

1 kg (2¼ lb) fresh tuna
1 onion, chopped
45 ml (3 tbsp) olive oil
1 aubergine (eggplant), peeled and diced like the fish
1 large tomato, skinned, seeded and chopped
8 black olives, stoned (pitted)
2 garlic cloves, chopped
Sprig of basil leaves, chopped
300 ml (½ pt · 1¼ cups) water
Salt and black freshly ground black pepper

1. Skin the tuna fish and cut it into 2.5 cm (1 in) cubes.

2. Place the fish in a casserole dish (Dutch oven). Add chopped onion, oil, aubergine, tomato, black olives, garlic and basil. Moisten with water or fish stock. Season with a little salt and a good pinch of black pepper. Cover with a lid and bake in the oven for 20 minutes at 200°C/400°F/gas mark 6. Serve hot from the dish with rice or cold with green salad.

 Rosé wine or dry cider are good accompaniments.

Preparation time: 20 minutes.
Cooking time: 20 minutes.

Scandinavian Fish Dumplings

These light dumplings make an excellent buffet party dish.

—————————— ∽ SERVES 4 to 6 ∾ ——————————

1 kg (2¼ lb) cod fillet
1 onion, finely chopped
30 ml (2 tbsp) white breadcrumbs
5 ml (1 tsp) sugar
1 egg
5 ml (1 tsp) salt
Pinch of white pepper
1 carrot, peeled and thinly sliced slantwise
1 onion, sliced
600 ml (1 pt · 2½ cups) water or fish stock
Juice of 1 lemon
1 sprig fennel or dill

1. Wash, drain and pat dry the skinless fish. Mince (grind) it then blend with the chopped onion, breadcrumbs, sugar, egg, salt and white pepper. Divide the mixture into 50 g/2 oz dumplings.

2. Half fill a casserole (Dutch oven) with the sliced carrot and onion. Add the water or fish stock. Place the dumplings in the dish. Add the lemon juice, fennel or dill. Season then cover with a lid and poach in the oven for 20 minutes at 200°C/400°F/gas mark 6. Serve hot or cold with sliced beetroot (red beet) and celery salad or with mangetout (snow peas).

 Hock, Alsace, or sparkling white wine to accompany.

Preparation time: 20 minutes.
Cooking time: 20 minutes.

Swedish-style Smoked Herring Casserole

If you can't find salted smoked herring, try using kipper fillets.

∾ SERVES 4 ∾

8 x 50 g (2 oz · ⅛ lb) salted smoked herring
450 g (1 lb · 4 cups) potatoes, thinly sliced
1 onion, sliced
300 ml (½ pt · 1¼ cups) single (light) cream
Juice of 1 lemon
Salt and black freshly ground black pepper
15 ml (1 tbsp) dill (dillweed), coarsely chopped

1. Wash the herring in cold running water for 15 minutes to remove the excess salt. Drain and pat dry.

2. Blanch the sliced potatoes for 2 minutes in boiling water and drain.

3. Place a layer of potatoes and raw onion in a casserole dish (Dutch oven). Cover with the herring pieces. Mix the lemon juice and cream, pour in half of the cream and cover with the remaining potatoes, onions and dill. Pour the remaining cream on top. Season to taste. Cover the casserole with a lid and bake at 180°C/350°F/gas mark 4 for 30 minutes.

 White Burgundy or light rosé wine to accompany.

Preparation time: 20 minutes.
Cooking time: 30 minutes.

Salmon Casserole
with Basmati Rice

Basmati rice has travelled from the foothills of the Himalayas. It has been tended and harvested by hand in an area whose soil and climatic characteristics give the rice its exquisite and delicate texture, flavour and aroma. Basmati means 'the fragrant one'. Easy-cook Basmati is the classic grain, pre-steamed to seal in the goodness, and guaranteed to produce fluffy, separate grains every time. In this dish you can enjoy the flavour of the Orient with the flavour of salmon. Scottish salmon is best but if you cannot find it, used farmed salmon instead.

_____ ∽ SERVES 3 to 4 ∾ _____

100 g (4 oz · ½ cup) Basmati rice
50 g (2 oz · ¼ cup) butter
1 shallot, chopped
Sprig of dill (dillweed), chopped
Juice of 1 lemon
Grated rind of ½ lemon
225 g (8 oz · 2 cups) skinned salmon cut into small pieces
300 ml (½ pt · 1¼ cups) water
Salt and freshly ground black pepper

1. Combine the rice and melted butter in a casserole dish (Dutch oven), then stir in the fish, shallot, dill, lemon juice and grated rind.
2. Pour in the water and season. Cover with a lid and bake at 200°C/400°F/gas mark 6 for 20–25 minutes. Serve with a cucumber salad blended with yoghurt and chopped fresh mint.

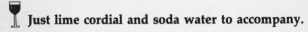

Just lime cordial and soda water to accompany.

Preparation time: 10 minutes.
Cooking time: 20–25 minutes.

Fillet of Sole with Grapes

A classic dish which is equally good with plaice fillets.

_____ ∾ SERVES 2 ∾ _____

4 x 75 g (3 oz) sole fillets
15 ml (1 tbsp) seasoned flour
50 g (2 oz · ¼ cup) butter, melted
1 shallot, chopped
150 ml (¼ pt · ⅔ cup) dry white wine
Salt and freshly ground black pepper
150 g (5 oz · scant 1 cup) seedless grapes
120 ml (4 fl oz · ½ cup) double (heavy) cream

1. Gently beat the sole fillets with a wooden mallet to prevent curling during cooking.
2. Coat the fillets in the seasoned flour, shaking off the surplus.
3. Put the melted butter and chopped shallot into a casserole dish (Dutch oven). Lay the sole fillets over the mixture and cover with white wine. Season to taste. Sprinkle seedless grapes on top. Put the lid on and bake at 200°C/400°F/gas mark 6 for 15–20 minutes. Blend cream into the fish liquor. Check seasoning and serve from the dish.

 Sancerre, Muscadet or Anjou wine to accompany.

Preparation time: 10 minutes.
Cooking time: 15–20 minutes.

Smoked Haddock and Potato Casserole

If you can find un-dyed smoked haddock, the flavour is superb.

1 kg (2¼ lb) smoked haddock fillet in 4 or 6 pieces
450 g (1 lb · 4 cups) potatoes, thinly sliced
50 g (2 oz · ¼ cup) butter, melted
Salt and freshly ground black pepper
300 ml (½ pt · 1¼ cups) water
2 garlic cloves, chopped
120 ml (4 fl oz · ½ cup) single (light) cream

1. Place the fish fillets in a casserole dish (Dutch oven) and cover with overlapping potato slices. Sprinkle over the melted butter, seasoning, water and garlic. Cover with a lid. Bake at 180°C/350°F/gas mark 4 for 35 minutes. Pour over the cream 5 minutes before the end of the cooking time. Return to the oven for the final 5 minutes. Serve from the dish.

 Dry cider or wine cup to accompany.

Preparation time: 15 minutes.
Cooking time: 35 minutes.

Greek-style Mackerel Casserole

This dish is best served at room temperature.

―――――――――― ∾ Serves 4 as a starter ∾ ――――――――――

4 mackerel fillets, cut into small pieces
300 ml (½ pt · 1¼ cups) dry white wine
45 ml (3 tbsp) olive oil
150 g (5 oz · 1¼ cups) spring onions (scallions), chopped
150 g (5 oz · ⅓ lb) button mushrooms
Fennel stalk, cut into small strips
Salt and 5 ml (1 tsp) crushed peppercorns
30 ml (2 tbsp) chopped parsley

1. Place the fish pieces in a casserole dish (Dutch oven) with all the ingredients except the parsley. Cover and bake in the oven at 200°C/400°F/gas mark 6 for 25 minutes. Cool and serve with a sprinkling of parsley.

 Bordeaux Blanc or Macon Blanc to accompany.

Preparation time: 10 minutes.
Cooking time: 25 minutes.

Prawn-stuffed Marrow Boats

This mixture makes a delicious stuffing for courgettes (zucchini) too.

────────── ∽ SERVES 4 as a hot starter ∽ ──────────

1 young marrow (squash), peeled
450 g (1 lb · 4 cups) peeled prawns (shrimp)
1 shallot, chopped
150 g (5 oz · 1¼ cups) carrots, grated
2.5 ml (½ tsp) dried mint
120 ml (4 fl oz · ½ cup) soured (dairy sour) cream
Salt and freshly ground black pepper
5 ml (1 tsp) curry powder
5 ml (1 tsp) paprika
100 g (4 oz · 1 cup) strong cheese, grated

1. Cut the marrow in half lengthwise. Remove the seeds with a spoon to form a cavity. Divide the marrow into four pieces. Boil in salted water in a casserole dish (Dutch oven) for no more than 6 minutes. Drain and return to casserole.

2. Combine the prawns with the shallot, carrot, mint, and cream. Season with salt, curry powder and paprika.

3. Fill the marrow boats with the prawn mixture. Sprinkle over the grated cheese. Bake uncovered hollow side up for 15 minutes until golden brown at 200°C/400°F/gas mark 6.

Hock or other German wine to accompany.

Preparation time: 15 minutes.
Cooking time: 15 minutes.

Halibut Fillets on a Bed of Spinach

This delicate oily fish goes very well with spinach. In order to preserve the precious minerals and flavour it is best to cook spinach without water.

————————— ∾ SERVES 2–4 ∾ —————————

450 g (1 lb) fresh spinach
150 ml (¼ pt · ⅔ cup) thick Greek yoghurt
4 fillets halibut, about 450 g (1 lb) in all
Salt and black freshly ground black pepper
Good pinch of grated nutmeg
2 garlic cloves, chopped
120 ml (4 lf oz · ½ cup) water
30 ml (2 tbsp) flaked peanuts, toasted

1. Wash the spinach in plenty of water. Drain and pat dry with a clean cloth. Gently squeeze out the surplus water.

2. Place the spinach in a deep casserole dish (Dutch oven).

3. Spread a thick coating of yoghurt over the fish fillets. Season to taste with salt, pepper and nutmeg. Arrange the fillets on top of the spinach leaves. Press down a little. Liquidise the garlic with the water. Pour over the fish. Sprinkle the peanuts over the fish. Cover with a lid and bake in the oven at 200°C/400°F/gas mark 6 for 20 minutes. Serve with boiled new potatoes or plain boiled rice.

 Chardonnay to accompany.

Preparation time: 15 minutes.
Cooking time: 20 minutes.

Indian-style Fish Casserole

In the rice fields of Asia, fish are reared in the waters of the paddy fields, ensuring a fresh supply of protein to eat with the rice. At the same time, in Europe, some fish has become more expensive than meat, hence the necessity of stretching fish with other ingredients, such as rice. So this Eastern recipe really meets the needs of Western cooks.

---------------------------------- ∾ SERVES 4 ∾ ----------------------------------

4 x 225 g (8 oz · ½ lb) fillets of haddock or pollack, with skin left on
Curry flour: (30 ml (2 tbsp) curry powder; 30 ml (2 tbsp) flour; 2
garlic cloves, chopped; 1 green chilli, chopped)
60 ml (4 tbsp) soya oil
6 bananas, peeled and sliced slantwise
6 large tomatoes, skinned, seeded, and chopped
15 ml (1 tbsp) desiccated (shredded) coconut
30 ml (2 tbsp) coriander (cilantro) leaves or parsley

1. Wash the fish fillets and pat dry. Coat in the curry flour. Heat the oil in a casserole (Dutch oven) and fry (sauté) the fish on one side only for 4 minutes. Fill the casserole dish with the sliced banana and chopped tomatoes. Sprinkle over the desiccated coconut. Cook in a hot oven 220°C/425°F/gas mark 7 for 12 minutes. Sprinkle over the chopped coriander leaves or parsley just before serving.

 Chilled lager to accompany.

Preparation time: 15 minutes.
Cooking time: 12 minutes.

Hake Hot Pot

For casseroles and hot pot recipes I recommend the use of a heavy casserole. Hake is probably one of the most tasty white fish we can eat. It can be prepared in the same way as cod, but has a firmer flesh and is delicious served cold with mayonnaise. I worked in a Boulogne fish restaurant owned by my family and this was one of the daily specialities.

―――――――――――― ∽ SERVES 4 OR 6 ∾ ――――――――――――

60 ml (4 tbsp) peanut (groundnut) oil
2 onions, chopped
1 celery stick, chopped
1 fennel bulb, chopped
450 g (1 lb · 4 cups) new potatoes, sliced
1 l (1¾ pts · 4¼ cups) water
Sprig of thyme
5 ml (1 tsp) salt
5 ml (1 tsp) freshly ground black pepper
1 kg (2¼ lb) hake, filleted, skinned and cut in 4 or 6 portions
4 tomatoes, skinned, seeded and chopped
45 ml (3 tbsp) chopped parsley

1. In a casserole (Dutch oven) heat the oil and fry (sauté) the onions, celery, and fennel for 4 minutes. Add the potatoes, water, and sprig of thyme. Season with the salt and pepper. Bake for 15 minutes at 200°C/400°F/gas mark 6. Remove the casserole from the oven and place the fish on top of the vegetables and cover with the chopped tomatoes. Put the lid on and bake for a further 8 minutes. Serve from the pot with a good sprinkling of parsley.

Lightly sparkling Portuguese rosé to accompany.

Preparation time: 20 minutes.
Cooking time: 23 minutes.

Salmon Steaks in Mustard Sauce

Extensive farming has resulted in producing salmon which is almost as cheap as cod. Boiled or grilled, salmon is always welcome. But there are other ways of cooking this fish which are a little bit more exciting. The combination of mustard, cream and dill goes well with this oily fish. As the central bone and skin are easily removed once cooked, and since they contribute to the flavour, I suggest they are left in during cooking. This dish may be served from individual casserole or gratin dishes, each with a 300 ml (½ pint · 1¼ cups) capacity.

∽ SERVES 4 ∾

---

50 g (2 oz · ¼ cup) butter
2 garlic cloves, chopped
8 shallots, chopped
4 x 225 g (8 oz · ½ lb) salmon steaks, washed and dried
Juice of 1 lemon
45 ml (3 tbsp) mild mustard
300 ml (½ pt · 1¼ cups) single (light) cream
Salt and freshly ground black pepper
30 ml (2 tbsp) chopped mixture of basil, mint, and parsley
45 ml (3 tbsp) dill (dillweed), chopped

1. Grease a large casserole (Dutch oven) or 4 individual gratin dishes with butter. Sprinkle in the garlic and shallots and place salmon steaks on top. Squeeze over a little lemon juice. Mix the mustard, cream, salt, black pepper, and all the herbs. Pour the mixture over the fish. Bake for 20 minutes at 180°C/350°F/gas mark 4.

2. Serve from the cooking dish with a cucumber salad.

 Sancerre or Muscadet to accompany.

Preparation time: 10 minutes.
Cooking time: 20 minutes.

Baked Bass with Walnut

This recipe is adaptable to any kind of fish (such as sea bass, grouper, grey mullet or bonito). The walnut sauce is extremely nutritious and makes a change from the French béchamel and velouté sauces.

─────────────── ∾ SERVES 4 ∾ ───────────────

1½ kg (3 lb) whole bass, filleted and skinned
450 g (1 lb · 4 cups) Jerusalem artichokes, sliced

Flavouring paste:
2 garlic cloves, chopped
30 ml (2 tbsp) coriander (cilantro) leaves, chopped
90 ml (6 tbsp) olive oil
Salt and freshly ground black pepper

Sauce:
150 g (5 oz · 1¼ cups) walnuts
Juice of 1 lemon
½ green chilli, seeded and chopped
30 ml (2 tbsp) olive oil
60 ml (4 tbsp) water
15-30 ml (1-2 tbsp) double (heavy) cream or yoghurt

1. To make the paste, pound the garlic and coriander with the olive oil and salt and pepper. Rub the fish fillets with this mixture.

2. Place the fish in a gratin earthenware dish. Cover with sliced Jerusalem artichokes. Cover with foil and bake for 20 minutes at 180°C/350°F/gas mark 4.

3. Meanwhile, prepare the sauce by pounding to a paste or liquidising the walnuts, lemon juice, chilli, olive oil, and water. A little cream or yoghurt may also be added. Serve the fish with the sauce handed separately.

 German Moselle to accompany.

Preparation time: 25 minutes.
Cooking time: 20 minutes.
34

Baked Sea Bream with Tahini Sauce

This Arab fish dish has an interesting flavour. The sea bream may be replaced by other fish such as trout, haddock, pollack, and cod.

_____ ∾ SERVES 4 ∾ _____

4 x 150 g (5 oz · 1/3 lb) sea bream, filleted and scaled

Garnish:
450 g (1 lb · 4 cups) onions, sliced
450 g (1 lb · 4 cups) new potatoes, sliced
Olive oil

Tahini Sauce:
150 g (5 oz · 1¼ cups) sesame seeds
300 ml (½ pt · 1¼ cups) water
Juice and rind of 2 lemons
2 garlic cloves, chopped
5 ml (1 tsp) salt
1 chilli, chopped
45 ml (3 tbsp) vinegar
30 ml (2 tbsp) snipped chives

1. In a pan heat the oil and stir fry the onions for 4 minutes without browning over a low heat.

2. Place the potatoes in the bottom of a casserole (Dutch oven) and cover with the onion. Place the fish on top and season with salt and pepper.

3. Pound the tahini sauce ingredients together in a pestle and mortar or purée in a blender or food processor. Spread the tahini over the fish. Cover with foil and bake for 20 minutes at 180°C/350°F/gas mark 4.

Retsina is the ideal accompaniment or a white Rioja.

Preparation time: 25 minutes.
Cooking time: 20 minutes.

Chapter Three

BEEF CASSEROLES

BRAISED OR POT ROASTED BEEF is usually made tender by soaking it in a marinade prior to cooking. Meat cuts taken from the forequarters of beef are tougher than those taken from the ribs, loin and rump. Meat is at its most succulent when the juice and cooking liquor have saturated the meat like a sponge. This point can only be reached through a slow cooking process; quick and fast boiling will not tenderise the meat. Before I discuss the benefits of using meat tenderisers, I would like to explain how meat is tenderised as it matures. Meat tends to be tougher immediately after slaughter. To tenderise the meat it is necessary to hang the carcass of beef for at least 14 days in a low temperature (1°C/34°F). During that time lactic acid is formed which preserves the meat and retards the growth of bacteria. The effects of rigor mortis are gradually reversed.

There are some tenderising powders on the market which are extracted from certain fruits which have the capacity to break down proteins. In this section I shall include in my recipes the use of fruits with such tenderising properties such as fresh pineapple, figs and pawpaws.

Prime Joints for Braising
from the Hindquarter

Topside, top rump and silverside are all excellent joints for pot roasting and braising. Because of the quality of the meat, they also tend to be more expensive. You will also see thick slices simply labelled *braising steak* in the supermarkets.

Prime Joints for Boiling and Stewing
from the Forequarter

Cuts that are suitable for boiling and stewing are usually less expensive. Look or ask for chuck steak, brisket, shin, leg or shank. You can also buy packs ready diced in the supermarket, called *stewing beef*, which are fine for any casserole.

We should bear in mind that there are many traditional stews which will remain very popular as long as high quality beef continues to be produced. Each dish will produce its own sauce which can be used elsewhere with vegetables or pasta.

Steak and Kidney Casserole

This is an old Royal Navy favourite from the war when I served as a cook to the First Lord of the Admiralty Submarine Command. The Port makes a real difference to this otherwise very ordinary stew – what a taste!

--- ∾ SERVES 6 ∾ ---

1 kg (2¼ lb) chuck steak cut into 2.5 cm (1 in) cubes
1 ox kidney, trimmed, fat removed and cut in small pieces
30 ml (2 tbsp) seasoned flour
15 ml (1 tbsp) mustard powder
30 ml (2 tbsp) oil
300 ml (½ pt · 1¼ cups) water
300 ml (½ pt · 1¼ cups) ruby port
1 onion, diced
1 carrot, diced
1 celery stick, diced
Salt and freshly ground black pepper
Pinch of dried thyme

1. Rub the meat with the combined seasoned flour and powdered mustard. In a casserole (Dutch oven), heat the oil and brown the meat for 10 minutes to sear in the juice. Then add the water, half the port, and all the remaining ingredients.

2. Transfer to the oven and braise for 1½ hours at 180°C/350°F/gas mark 4. Near the end of the cooking time, about 15 minutes before the meat is done, add the remaining port and a pinch of ground thyme. Cover with a lid and cook for the last 15 minutes.

Serve with jacket baked potatoes or with creamed cauliflower and carrots.

Red Spanish wine to accompany.

Preparation time: 20 minutes.
Cooking time: 1½ hours.

Rich Beef Stew

This recipe is based on a rich Parisian dish famed in France for its succulence. The meat is taken from the rump, cut to 1 cm (½ in) thick.

―――――――――― ∽ SERVES 4 ∽ ――――――――――

4 x 225 g (8 oz · ½ lb) braising steaks
50 g (2 oz · ¼ cup) seasoned flour
45 ml (3 tbsp) oil
150 ml (¼ pt · ⅔ cup) medium Madeira
300 ml (½ pt · 1¼ cups) beef stock
450 g (1 lb) button mushrooms
450 g (1 lb) button onions
225 g (8 oz · 1½ cups) stuffed olives
5 ml (1 tsp) honey
1 garlic clove, crushed
15 ml (1 tbsp) tomato purée (paste)
2.5 ml (½ tsp) dried tarragon
Salt and freshly ground black pepper

1. Coat the steaks in the seasoned flour and shake off the surplus. Heat the oil in a casserole dish (Dutch oven) and brown the steaks for 3 minutes on each side. Remove the surplus oil and add all the remaining ingredients. Bring to the boil.

2. Transfer to the oven at 180°C/350°F/gas mark 4 for 1¾–2 hours. Add a little more water or Madeira during cooking as necessary to keep meat bathed in sauce.

Serve with French beans or flageolet.

Beaujolais or very dry Madeira wine to accompany.

Preparation time: 15 minutes.
Cooking time: 1¾–2 hours.

Beefburger Casserole German-style

Braised beefburgers are probably tastier cooked in their own juice than fried or grilled. This type of burger is highly seasoned and enriched with eggs and fresh herbs.

―――――――――――― ∽ SERVES 4 OR 8 ∾ ――――――――――――

Burger mixture:
1 kg (2¼ lb · 9 cups) lean minced (ground) beef
1 onion, chopped
1 egg, beaten
45 ml (3 tbsp) chopped parsley
5 ml (1 tsp) caraway seeds (optional)
50 g (2 oz · 1 cup) white breadcrumbs
Salt and freshly ground black pepper
45 ml (3 tbsp) oil

Vegetable garnish:
450 g (1 lb · 4 cups) carrots, very thinly sliced
1 onion, sliced
1 celery stick, sliced
300 ml (½ pt · 1¼ cups) strong brown German beer
300 ml (½ pt · 1¼ cups) water
5 ml (1 tsp) clear honey
Salt, black pepper and ground mace

1. In a casserole (Dutch oven), combine all the beefburger mixture ingredients except the oil. Divide into 8 balls. Flatten slightly. The burgers must be 2.5 cm (1 in) thick.

2. Heat the oil in the casserole. Brown the burgers for 5 minutes. Discard the surplus oil. Add the vegetable garnish, beer, water, honey and seasoning. Cover with a lid and gently braise in the oven at 180°C/350°F/gas mark 4 for 1 hour.

 Strong brown German beer is ideal, or lager if you prefer.

Preparation time: 30 minutes.
Cooking time: 1 hour.

Beef and Bramley Casserole

Apple and beef make a good combination, contrasting in taste and texture with the cabbage and other ingredients in this dish. It is important to sear the meat to increase the beefy taste.

$\sim$ SERVES 4 $\sim$

4 braising steaks from topside
50 g (2 oz · ½ cup) seasoned flour
45 ml (3 tbsp) oil
half green cabbage, shredded
4 large cooking (tart) apples, cored, and sliced
1 onion, thinly sliced
300 ml (½ pt · 1¼ cups) water or dry cider
Salt and freshly ground black pepper
5 ml (1 tsp) caraway seeds
15 ml (1 tbsp) brown sugar

1. Coat the steak with the seasoned flour and shake off the surplus.

2. Heat the oil in casserole dish (Dutch oven) and fry (sauté) meat for 5 minutes until brown on both sides. Remove the surplus oil and add the cabbage, apples, onion and water or cider. Bring to the boil then season with salt, pepper and sugar and add caraway seeds. Cover with a lid and braise in the oven for 1½ hours at 180°C/350°F/gas mark 4.

 Cider is the best drink to accompany this tasty casserole.

Preparation time: 20 minutes.
Cooking time: 1½ hours.

Meat Loaf with Leeks

This is a very cheap yet tender beef dish, made from minced meat
bound with eggs and mixed herbs and cooked with leeks.

---------------- ∾ SERVES 4–6 ∾ ----------------

1 kg (2¼ lb · 9 cups) minced (ground) beef
1 egg, beaten
50 g (2 oz · 1 cup) breadcrumbs
30 ml (2 tbsp) chopped mixture of parsley, basil and chives
5 ml (1 tsp) salt
1.5 ml (¼ tsp) freshly ground black pepper
45 ml (3 tbsp) oil
15 g (½ oz · 1 tbsp) butter
3 leeks, white part only, sliced
300 ml (½ pt · 1¼ cups) white wine

1. In a casserole (Dutch oven) blend the minced beef with the
egg, breadcrumbs and herbs. Season with salt and pepper. Put the
mixture on a floured board and form a thick roll 6 cm (2½ in)
diameter.

2. Heat the oil and butter in the casserole and add the leeks. Put
the meat roll on top of the layer of leeks. Pour the wine over and
season. Braise uncovered at 200°C/400°F/gas mark 6 for 45
minutes. The meat loaf should be lightly brown. Baste it with wine
from time to time. Serve cut into four thick slices.

 Dry cider or lager to accompany.

Preparation time: 15 minutes.
Cooking time: 45 minutes.

Chinese Beef with Almonds

The Chinese style of cooking is quick and easy for amateur cooks to master. In this dish, I have adapted an old stir-fry recipe using a cheaper cut of meat. The secret lies in marinating the beef before it is cooked.

_____ ∽ SERVES 4–6 ∽ _____

1 kg (2¼ lb) thick beef flank
5 ml (1 tsp) cornflour (cornstarch)
300 ml (½ pt · 1¼ cups) water
100 g (4 oz · 1 cup) almonds

Marinade:
150 ml (¼ pt · ⅔ cup) pineapple juice
15 ml (1 tbsp) clear honey
15 ml (1 tbsp) soy sauce
1 small piece peeled ginger
1 garlic clove
1 onion
10 ml (2 tbsp) oil
15 ml (1 tbsp) sherry vinegar
Salt and freshly ground black pepper
Pinch of five-spice powder
1 small piece chilli, seeded and chopped

1. Cut the meat into very thin strips 4 cm (1½ in) long and 1 cm (½ in) thick.

2. Liquidise the marinade ingredients. Pour into a casserole dish (Dutch oven). Add the meat, cover and leave in the fridge for 2 hours.

3. Mix the cornflour and water. Season and stir into the casserole. Braise for 1 hour at 180°C/350°F/gas mark 4. After 20 minutes give the mixture a good stir. Taste and add salt. Continue braising, adding a little water if the liquid evaporates too quickly. Add the almonds 10 minutes before the end of cooking. Serve with noodles or spaghetti.

 Saké to accompany.

Preparation time: 15 minutes plus marinating time.
Cooking time: 1 hour.

Beef in Red Wine

Silverside or a boned rib joint are equally good for this casserole, where the meat is be cooked in one piece as a braised joint.

──────────── ∾ SERVES 4–6 ∾ ────────────

45 ml (3 tbsp) oil
1 kg (2¼ lb) silverside joint
300 ml (½ pt · 1¼ cups) red wine
300 ml (½ pint · 1¼ cups) beef stock or water with a beef stock cube
45 ml (1 tbsp) tomato purée (paste)
Sprig of thyme
Salt and freshly ground black pepper
5 ml (1 tsp) cornflour (cornstarch)
120 ml (4 fl oz · ½ cup) cold water

Garnish:
8 small onions
8 small carrots

1. In a casserole (Dutch oven) heat the oil and brown the meat all over for 6 minutes. Remove the surplus oil and transfer to the oven at 200°C/400°F/gas mark 6. Cook for 30 minutes then reduce the heat to 180°C/350°F/gas mark 4. Add the red wine, beef stock or water, tomato purée, sprig of thyme and garnish. Season and cover with a lid and cook gently for 1½ hours. During cooking maintain the level of liquid by adding water. Turn the joint over once or twice.

2. Remove the meat and garnish from the casserole. Keep warm. Blend the cornflour and water together. Stir into the casserole. Bring to the boil, stirring until thickened and glossy. Season the sauce and remove the thyme. To serve, carve the meat into thin slices and accompany with the garnish and green vegetables.

 Red Bulgarian or Australian Cabernet to accompany.

Preparation time: 15 minutes.
Cooking time: 2 hours.

Ox Heart, Celery and Parsnip Casserole

This kind of offal is extremely nourishing but requires long, slow cooking to make it tender and tasty.

─── ∾ SERVES 4–6 ∾ ───

1 kg (2¼ lb) ox heart
50 g (2 oz · ½ cup) seasoned flour
45 ml (3 tbsp) oil
225 g (8 oz · 2 cups) rindless back bacon, diced
4 parsnips, peeled and sliced
4 celery sticks, sliced
1 onion, sliced
15 ml (1 tbsp) tomato purée (paste)
600 ml (1 pt · 2½ cups) water or flat lager (beer)
5 ml (1 tsp) yeast extract
Salt and freshly ground black pepper

1. Remove the blood vessels and surplus fat from the heart. Split it in two and cut into thin slices. Coat in the seasoned flour.

2. Heat the oil in a casserole (Dutch oven) and brown the meat and bacon for 5 minutes. Add the vegetables, tomato purée, water or beer, yeast extract and seasoning. Cover with a lid, bring the liquid to the boil and boil for 5 minutes. Then transfer to the oven and braise at 180°C/350°F/gas mark 4 on the middle shelf for 2 hours. After one hour check that there is enough liquid and add water if necessary.

Serve with boiled potatoes and green cabbage.

 Dry cider or lager to accompany.

Preparation time: 25 minutes.
Cooking time: 2 hours.

47

Ox Liver in Stout

This is the toughest type of liver and so requires slow cooking at a low temperature. To increase its tenderness the liver can be marinated in a mixture containing fresh pineapple juice for 2 hours. The enzyme in the juice will begin to break down the liver protein and make it more digestible. Soaking the liver in water with salt for 2 hours also helps to eliminate the blood and bleaches the liver to a more attractive, pale colour.

―――――――――――――― ∾ SERVES 4–6 ∾ ――――――――――――――

1 kg (2¼ lb) ox liver
150 ml (¼ pt · ⅔ cup) fresh pineapple juice
50 g (2 oz · ½ cup) seasoned flour
45 ml (3 tbsp) oil
225 g (8 oz · 2 cups) rindless streaky bacon, diced
2 garlic cloves, chopped
30 ml (2 tbsp) soy sauce
1 small piece of root ginger (ginger root), grated
300 ml (½ pt · 1¼ cups) stout or brown beer
300 ml (½ pt · 1¼ cups) water
1 onion, diced
Salt and freshly ground black pepper
2.5 ml (½ tsp) ground mace

1. Cut the liver into 1 cm (½ in) cubes. Place in a casserole (Dutch oven) and cover with the pineapple juice. Marinate for 2 hours, turning from time to time. Drain and pat dry. Coat with seasoned flour. Discard the pineapple juice. Dry the casserole with kitchen towel.

2. Heat the oil in the casserole and quickly brown the liver and bacon for 5 minutes.

3. Liquidise the garlic, soy sauce and ginger with 60 ml (4 tbsp) of water. Add to the liver along with the stout, water and onion. Season with salt, pepper and ground mace. Braise in the oven slowly at 180°C/350°F/gas mark 4 for 1½-2 hours. Maintain the level of liquid by adding water as it evaporates. Check the seasoning before serving with boiled rice or pasta.

Red Bulgarian wine or pineapple juice cup to accompany.

Preparation time: 15 minutes plus marinating time.
Cooking time: 1½–2 hours.

Steak Casserole with Beans

This is a hot-pot casserole that's as old as the Incas and is still often served in Latin American countries. The beef skirt is the part attached to the spinal column, trimmed of excess fat and connective tissue.

Distilled water is best for soaking dried beans. The insoluble minerals in hard tap water stick to them, forming a coating.

───────────────── ∽ SERVES 4 ∽ ─────────────────

225 g (8 oz · 2 cups) dried haricot (navy) beans, soaked overnight in
distilled water
4 carrots, peeled and trimmed
4 onions, chopped
1 celery stick
1 l (1¾ pts · 4¼ cups) water
Sprig of thyme
1 kg (2¼ lb) beef skirt
Salt and freshly ground black pepper

1. Place the soaked beans in a casserole (Dutch oven) with the carrots, onions, celery and water. Bring the liquid to the boil and remove the scum as it rises. Boil rapidly for 10 minutes. Add the thyme.

2. Cut the beef skirt into small steaks. Place on top of the beans and season only with pepper. Cover with a lid and braise in the oven at 180°C/350°F/gas mark 4 for 2¼ hours. Season with salt at the last minute. Check and adjust the liquid level during cooking.

Serve hot with pickled gherkins, chutney and beetroot (red beet) salad.

 Red or rosé wine from Provence to accompany.

Preparation time: 15 minutes plus soaking time.
Cooking time: 2¼ hours.

Braised Cabbage Parcels with Beef Stuffing

You need green cabbage leaves for this dish which is very nourishing and tasty. It is particularly good when served with a tomato and garlic sauce.

───────────── ∾ SERVES 4 ∾ ─────────────

8 green cabbage leaves, with central stalk removed
2 large tomatoes, skinned, seeded and chopped
300 ml (½ pt · 1¼ cups) water
Salt and freshly ground black pepper

Stuffing:
450 g (1 lb · 4 cups) minced (ground) beef
1 onion, chopped
1 garlic clove, chopped
1 egg, beaten
30 ml (2 tbsp) chopped parsley
50 g (2 oz · ½ cup) seasoned flour

1. Blanch the cabbage leaves and refresh in cold water. Drain and pat dry. Spread them on a clean cloth.

2. In a casserole (Dutch oven), combine all the stuffing ingredients. Divide into eight balls. Place one ball on each cabbage leaf. Wrap the cabbage around the ball. Place the parcels in the casserole dish. Cover with chopped tomatoes and add water and seasoning. Cover with a lid and braise for 1¾ hours at 180°C/350°F/gas mark 4.

 Rosé d'Anjou or Spanish rosé to accompany.

Preparation time: 20 minutes.
Cooking time: 1¾ hours.

French Beef Olives

This dish is so called because the stuffed rolls are shaped like olives..This is the French version my father used to prepare in his own restaurant in Boulogne.

─────────────── ∾ SERVES 8 ∾ ───────────────

8 x 225 g (8 oz · ½ lb) thin steaks from topside or top rump of beef
30 ml (2 tbsp) oil
4 carrots, sliced
4 small turnips, sliced
300 ml (½ pt · 1¼ cups) red wine
30 ml (2 tbsp) tomato purée (paste)
15 ml (1 tbsp) cornflour (cornstarch)

Filling:
450 g (1 lb · 4 cups) pork sausagemeat
30 ml (2 tbsp) chopped parsley
30 ml (2 tbsp) stoned (pitted) green olives, chopped
1 egg, beaten
30 ml (2 tbsp) flour

1. Mix together all the filling ingredients and divide into 8 portions.

2. Beat the steaks with a wooden mallet until they are as thin as escalopes and have a wide area on which to place the stuffing. Trim each steak to an oval. Place a portion of filling on each slice of beef and wrap it to make an oval shape. Tie up the ends with cook's string.

3. Heat the oil in a casserole (Dutch oven) and brown the beef olives for 8 minutes. Lift out then add the carrots and turnips and place the beef olives on top. Pour over the wine, just enough water to cover and add the tomato purée. Season and cover. Braise in the oven for 1½ hours at 180°C/350°F/gas mark 4.

4. When ready, remove the string and serve the beef olives on a bed of rice. Blend the cornflour with a little water. Stir into the gravy. Boil for 2 minutes stirring until thickened and clear. Season to taste and serve handed separately with the beef olives.

 Beaujolais or Macon to accompany.

Preparation time: 30 minutes.
Cooking time: 1½ hours.

Poached Beef with Vegetables

This is my version of the classic French dish, *Boef à la Mode*. It is delicious served hot or cold.

60 ml (4 tbsp) oil
1.5 kg (3 lb) whole piece of topside as a joint tied up in string
2 calves' feet, split (optional)
1 carrot, unpeeled, cut into chunks
1 white of leek, trimmed
1 onion, cut into quarters
300 ml (½ pt · 1¼ cups) dry white wine
1 piece bacon rind
2 beef stock cubes
600 ml (1 pt · 2½ cups) water
1 celery stick, sliced
2 garlic cloves, chopped
15 ml (1 tbsp) tomato purée (paste)
1 small bunch of tarragon
15 ml (1 tbsp) cornflour (cornstarch) with 45 ml (3 tbsp) water
600 ml (1 pt · 2½ cups) of the cooking liquor
Salt and freshly ground black pepper
2 carrots, cut in sticks
2 turnips, cut in sticks
225 g (8 oz · ½ lb) French beans, trimmed and cut to equal size
100 g (4 oz · ½ cup) butter for vegetable garnish
30 ml (2 tbsp) chopped parsley

1. Heat the oil in a casserole (Dutch oven) and brown the joint and calves' feet all over for 15 minutes.

2. Remove the joint and feet and brown the carrot, leek and onion for 5 minutes. Return the meat to the pot and add the wine, bacon rind and calves' feet. Crumble in a stock cube and add water.

3. Cover with a lid. Bring to the boil and transfer to the oven at 180°C/350°F/gas mark 4 for 2 hours.

4. Remove the joint. Rest on a dish and discard the string. Discard bones from the calves' feet and dice the meat.

5. Strain the cooking juices and return to the casserole. Boil it with the celery, garlic, tomato purée and tarragon for 5 minutes.

6. Blend together the cornflour and water with a cupful of the cooking sauce and add to the saucepan. Cook for a further 4 minutes. Strain and season.

7. To prepare the garnish if using. Boil the vegetables in salted water for 10 minutes. Rinse in hot water and serve separately with butter and parsley.

8. If serving hot, carve the meat thinly and serve with the diced calves' feet meat. Some people like it with French dressing.

If the meat is to be served cold, simply put it in a deep dish and cover completely with the sauce which will form a jelly on cooling. Mix the vegetable garnish in mayonnaise and serve with lettuce leaves.

 Rosé or Provence wine to accompany.

Preparation time: 30 minutes plus garnish if using.
Cooking time: 2 hours.

Beef in Beer

This dish orginated in Belgium and has become popular in countries where beer is a national drink. Not all beers are suitable: in my experience, I have found that Guinness or dark German stouts give the best flavour.

───────────── ∾ SERVES 6 ∾ ─────────────

1.5 kg (3 lb) topside or silverside of beef
50 g (2 oz · ½ cup) seasoned flour
60 ml (4 tbsp) oil
450 g (1 lb · 4 cups) onions, sliced
600 ml (1 pt · 2½ cups) dark stout or Guinness
15 ml (1 tbsp) malt vinegar
25 g (1 oz · 2 tbsp) brown sugar or honey
300 ml (½ pt · 1¼ cups) water
1 celery stick, chopped
Salt and freshly ground black pepper
2.5 ml (½ tsp) ground mace
Sprig of thyme

1. Cut the meat into 6 large thick slices. Coat in the seasoned flour.

2. In a casserole (Dutch oven) heat the oil and fry (sauté) the steaks for 2 minutes on each side. Remove from the dish.

3. In the same casserole heat the remaining oil and stir fry the onions for 2 minutes. Pour in the stout, malt vinegar, sugar and water and boil for 2 minutes. Add the meat with the thyme and celery. Season with the salt, pepper and ground mace and cover with a lid. Braise for 1½ hours at 180°C/350°F/gas mark 4.

 Beer, ale or stout to accompany.

Preparation time: 15 minutes.
Cooking time: 1½ hours.

Hungarian Beef Goulash

Traditionally the potatoes are cooked separately and added just before serving. But for quickness, cook in the goulash.

————————————— $\sim$ Serves 6 $\sim$ —————————————

50 g (2 oz · ½ cup) flour
15 ml (1 tbsp) mild paprika
60 ml (4 tbsp) oil
1.5 kg (3 lb) flank of beef, cut in 2.5 cm (1 in) cubes
150 g (5 oz · ⅔ cup) onions
600 ml (1 pt · 2½ cups) water
15 ml (1 tbsp) tomato purée (paste)
2.5 ml (½ tsp) allspice
5 ml (1 tsp) salt
450 g (1 lb) small new potatoes, scrubbed
30 ml (2 tbsp) chopped parsley

1. Sift the flour and paprika together and use to coat the beef. Heat the oil in a casserole dish (Dutch oven) and brown the meat for 5 minutes. Add the onions and cook for 2 minutes. Then blend in the water, tomato purée, allspice and salt. Add the potatoes.

2. Cover with a lid and bake in oven for 1½ hours at 180°C/350°F/gas mark 4. Check and adjust the liquid level.

3. Sprinkle with parsley before serving.

A robust Hungarian red wine to accompany.

Preparation time: 15 minutes.
Cooking time: 1½ hours.

Austrian Beef Casserole with Horseradish Sauce

The horseradish sauce will also transform smoked mackerel into an elegant party dish.

∾ SERVES 6 ∾

1 kg (2¼ lb) stewing beef
50 ml (2 fl oz · 3½ tbsp) oil
6 onions, sliced
1.5 l (2½ pts · 6 cups) water
3 beef stock cubes
bouquet garni
6 leeks

For the horseradish sauce:
150 ml (¼ pt · ⅔ cup) water
25 ml (1½ tbsp) white vinegar
175 g (6 oz · ⅓ lb) horseradish, scraped
175 g (6 oz · ⅓ lb) cooking (tart) apples, peeled and cored
25 g (1 oz · ½ cup) fresh white breadcrumbs
50 ml (2 fl oz · 3½ tbsp) single (light) cream

1. Cut the meat into 4 cm (1½ in) cubes.
2. Heat the oil in a casserole (Dutch oven) and brown the meat, covered with a lid, for 8 minutes, stirring frequently.
3. Add the onions to the meat, and brown for 3 minutes.
4. Cover with the water mixed with the beef stock cubes and bouquet garni.
5. Wash the leeks, cut into four lengthwise, tie in a bundle and put into the casserole with the meat.
6. Bring to the boil, and remove the scum as it rises to the surface. Simmer for 2–2½ hours on top of the stove or in the oven at 160°C/325°F/gas mark 3 until the meat is tender.

7. Meanwhile, put the water and vinegar in a bowl and grate the horseradish and apple into it. Soak for 1 hour. Drain off the liquid and mix the breadcrumbs and cream into the mixture. Place in a serving bowl.

8. When the meat is cooked, strain the broth off and serve separately as a soup. Remove the leeks, discard the string and place on top of the meat.

Serve with rice or noodles.

 Austrian Hock to accompany.

Preparation time: 30 minutes.
Cooking time: 2½ hours.

Casserole of Beef Sausages in Peanut Sauce

When sausages are freshly made, there is no better or more economical dish. This recipe can be prepared within 15 minutes and the addition of peanut sauce makes it a firm favourite with children.

⟳ SERVES 4 ⟳

---

30 ml (2 tbsp) oil
8 large beef sausages

Peanut sauce:
100 g (4 oz · 1 cup) salted peanuts, ground to powder
15 ml (1 tbsp) tomato ketchup (catsup)
5 ml (1 tsp) yeast extract
300 ml (½ pt · 1¼ cups) water
Juice of 1 orange
Salt and freshly ground black pepper

1. In a casserole (Dutch oven) heat the oil and brown the sausages all over for 4 minutes. Remove the surplus oil.
2. Stir in the peanut sauce ingredients. Cover with a lid and braise for 12 minutes at 200°C/400°F/gas mark 6.

 Muscadet or Beaujolais to accompany.

Preparation time: 5 minutes.
Cooking time: 12 minutes.

Peanut and Beef Casserole

Peanuts, or groundnuts as they are known in Africa, are a major source of protein for many people who cannot afford meat. For this dish use fresh, shelled peanuts crushed or coarsely chopped. Roasting them a little enhances the flavour. The stew can be served hot or cold with lettuce leaves as a sandwich filler.

───────────────── ∞ SERVES 4 ∞ ─────────────────

60 ml (4 tbsp) peanut (groundnut) oil
1 onion, chopped
1 green chilli, seeded and chopped
450 g (1 lb · 4 cups) shin of beef, cut into 1 cm (½ in) cubes
15 ml (1 tbsp) tomato purée (paste)
Pulp and juice of a fresh fig
150 g (5 oz · 1¼ cups) peanuts (groundnuts), ground
600 ml (1 pt · 2½ cups) water
5 ml (1 tsp) fresh root ginger (ginger root), chopped
Salt and freshly ground black pepper
30 ml (2 tbsp) chopped basil
2 green bananas, peeled and sliced

1. Heat the oil in a flameproof casserole (Dutch oven). Stir-fry the onions, chilli, and beef for 8 minutes. Add the tomato purée, fig, peanuts and water. Season. Bring to the boil and cover.

2. Cook on a low heat on top of the stove for 1½ hours. Check and adjust the level of liquid during cooking. Season to taste with salt, pepper and basil adding the ginger halfway through the cooking. Add the sliced bananas a few minutes before the dish has finished cooking.

Serve with rice.

 Red Bordeaux to accompany.

Preparation time: 20 minutes.
Cooking time: 1½ hours.

Chapter Four

VEAL CASSEROLES

THE FRENCH AND ITALIANS LOVE VEAL. There are hundreds of variations on veal escalopes from *schnitzels* to *scalopine Marsala*, while the French prefer braised veal chops and casseroled sweetbreads. In Britain there is still a preference for veal and ham pie and calves' liver (the most tender of the offals, but also the dearest).

Veal, being tender, does not require as long a cooking time as beef but it is the addition of an appropriate sauce that makes the veal tasty as the meat can be rather bland on its own.

Less expensive cuts from the forequarters are used for braising, pot roasting and for pies. Knuckles, breast and trotters are great delicacies as are the head, tongue and brain.

Stuffed Veal Breast

For a change, try this stuffing between two boned breasts of lamb, sewn up and cooked as below.

_____ ∽ SERVES 8 ∾ _____

2 kg (4½ lb) breast of veal, boned with cavity opened for stuffing

Stuffing:
100 g (4 oz · 1 cup) cooked rice
100 g (4 oz · 1 cup) beef sausagemeat
1 onion, chopped
30 ml (2 tbsp) chopped parsley
2 eggs
Salt and freshly ground black pepper

Veal Gravy:
45 ml (3 tbsp) oil
1 carrot, chopped
1 onion, chopped
1 stick celery, chopped
600 ml (1 pt · 2½ cups) water
2 stock cubes
15 ml (1 tbsp) cornflour (cornstarch) and 45 ml (3 tbsp) water

1. In a casserole (Dutch oven), combine all stuffing ingredients and fill the pocket inside the breast of veal. Sew up and season.

2. Heat the oil in the casserole and brown the meat all over for 15 minutes. Add the carrot, onion and celery. Add the water and crumble in the stock cubes. Cover and braise in the oven at 180°C/350°F/gas mark 4 for 2½ hours.

3. Remove the joint and vegetables. Blend the cornflour and cold water, stir into the gravy and boil for 4 minutes on top of the cooker. Season to taste and strain.

 Muscadet or Sancerre (Loire) wine to accompany.

Preparation time: 30 minutes.
Cooking time: 2½ hours.

Veal with Garlic Sauce

Garlic has certain medicinal and hedonic properties well known to gourmets. In this recipe the garlic is boiled without being skinned. It is then peeled and the pulp is puréed and diluted in the sauce. Because the garlic is boiled separately first, it isn't strictly a one-pot dish, but is so good I simply had to put it in anyway!

--- ∾ SERVES 4–6 ∾ ---

50 g (2 oz · ¼ cup) oil and butter combined
1.5 kg (3 lb) stewing veal, cut into 1 cm (½ in) cubes
1 onion, chopped
300 ml (½ pt · 1¼ cups) veal stock
120 ml (4 fl oz · ½ cup) dry Madeira
Salt and freshly ground black pepper
Pinch of paprika and pinch of chilli powder
1 bulb of garlic, unpeeled
1 egg yolk
120 ml (4 fl oz · ½ cup) single (light) cream
5 ml (1 tsp) cornflour (cornstarch)

1. In a casserole (Dutch oven) heat the oil and butter and brown the veal and the onion for 5 minutes stirring occasionally. Add the veal stock, Madeira and seasoning.

2. Divide the bulb of garlic and boil the cloves in water for 10 minutes. Peel and purée the garlic cloves and add to the veal. Simmer for 1½ hours. In a cup, blend the egg yolk, cream and the cornflour. Stir a little of the veal stock into this mixture and add to the casserole. Check the seasoning. Simmer for another 15 minutes.

Serve with shell pasta or rice.

 Muscadet or Hock to accompany.

Preparation time: 30 minutes.
Cooking time: 1¾ hours.

Braised Veal with Cognac

This is a very fragrant dish, particularly good for a dinner party.

1.25 kg (2¾ lb) piece of roasting veal from leg, cushion or undercushion
Pinch of paprika
2.5 ml (½ tsp) cinnamon
Salt and freshly ground black pepper
50 g (2 oz · ¼ cup) butter and oil combined
6 small onions
6 small carrots
1 l (1¾ pts · 4¼ cups) water
120 ml (4 fl oz · ½ cup) double (heavy) cream
15 ml (1 tbsp) cornflour (cornstarch) and 75 ml (5 tbsp) water combined
50 ml (2 fl oz · 3½ tbsp) cognac or brandy
30 ml (2 tbsp) chopped mint

1. Season the veal and rub paprika, cinnamon and salt all over the meat. Heat the butter and oil in a casserole dish (Dutch oven) and brown all over for 15 minutes. Add the onions and carrots, pour in the water and cover. Simmer in the oven for 1½ hours at 180°C/350°F/gas mark 4. Then remove the joint and vegetables and place the casserole on top of the stove and add the cream. Bring to the boil.

2. Add the cornflour and water to the sauce whisking continuously. Bring to the boil. Check the seasoning. Add the brandy and sprinkle in the mint leaves. Slice the veal and coat it with sauce.

Serve with rice, new potatoes or cauliflower.

 Sancerre or Macon Blanc to accompany.

Preparation time: 25 minutes.
Cooking time: 1½ hours.

Sautéed Veal in Tomato Sauce

This dish is equally good with lean lamb.

_____ ∾ SERVES 6 ∾ _____

60 ml (4 tbsp) oil
1 kg (2¼ lb) veal from shoulder, cut into 2.5 cm (1 in) cubes
1 onion, chopped
3 garlic cloves, chopped
45 ml (3 tbsp) flour
300 ml (½ pt · 1¼ cups) dry white wine
600 ml (1 pt · 2½ cups) water
4 large tomatoes, skinned, seeded and chopped
15 ml (1 tbsp) tomato purée (paste)
2.5 ml (½ tsp) sugar
Salt and freshly ground black pepper
15 ml (1 tbsp) chopped tarragon

1. Heat the oil in a casserole (Dutch oven) and brown the meat for 15 minutes. Add the onion and garlic and toss for 2 minutes. Sprinkle in the flour and add the wine, water, tomatoes, tomato purée, sugar, seasoning and tarragon.

2. Boil for 5 minutes then simmer for 1½ hours in an oven heated to 180°C/350°F/gas mark 4. Maintain the sauce level by adding wine or water as necessary. Check and adjust the seasoning.

Serve with rice or pasta or new boiled potatoes.

 Spanish rosé or Provence wine to accompany.

Preparation time: 25 minutes.
Cooking time: 1½ hours.

Italian-style Veal Casserole

Any cut of leg of veal can be used for this casserole dish.

—————————————— ∞ SERVES 6 ∞ ——————————————

1 kg (2¼ lb) braising veal, diced
50 g (2 oz · ½ cup) seasoned flour
45 ml (3 tbsp) olive oil
120 ml (4 fl oz · ½ cup) sweet white vermouth
450 g (1 lb · 4 cups) tomatoes, skinned, seeded and chopped
300 ml (½ pt · 1¼ cups) water
1 onion, chopped
1 fennel bulb, chopped
15 ml (1 tbsp) chopped tarragon
Salt and freshly ground black pepper

1. Coat the veal with the seasoned flour and shake off the surplus.

2. Heat the oil in a casserole (Dutch oven) and brown the veal all over for 5–8 minutes. Remove the surplus oil and add the vermouth, tomatoes, water, onions, fennel and tarragon. Season to taste. Cover with a lid and braise gently for 1½ hours at 180°C/350°F/gas mark 4.

Serve with peas or mangetout (snow peas).

 White Chianti to accompany.

Preparation time: 15 minutes.
Cooking time: 1½ hours.

French-style Sweetbread Casserole

Sweetbreads are delicious very tender and nourishing glands taken from throat and heart regions (thymus and pancreas). They should be cleaned and trimmed of all covering membranes before cooking.

―――――――――――――― ∾ SERVES 2 ∾ ――――――――――――――

2 whole calves' sweetbreads
5 ml (1 tsp) vinegar
50 g (2 oz · ½ cup) seasoned flour
45 ml (3 tbsp) oil and butter mixed
12 button mushrooms
12 button onions
300 ml (½ pt · 1¼ cups) dry white wine
100 ml (3½ fl oz · 6½ tbsp) double (heavy) cream
Salt and freshly ground black pepper

1. Parboil the sweetbreads in water in a casserole (Dutch oven) with the vinegar for 5 minutes. Discard the water.

2. Cool slightly and remove the covering membrane. Coat the sweetbreads in seasoned flour.

3. In the casserole heat the oil and butter and brown the sweetbreads for 5 minutes all over. Remove any surplus fat and add the mushrooms, onions, white wine, cream and seasoning. Braise uncovered for 35 minutes, basting from time to time.

Serve without any other garnish.

 Dry white wine to accompany.

Preparation time: 15 minutes.
Cooking time: 35 minutes.

Stuffed Heart Casserole

Vary the stuffing with ham and mushrooms instead of sausagemeat.

───────── ∼ SERVES 2–3 ∼ ─────────

1 calf's heart, weighing 450 g (1 lb), trimmed
30 ml (2 tbsp) butter or oil
Salt and freshly ground black pepper

Stuffing:
100 g (4 oz) beef sausagemeat
50 g (2 oz · 1 cup) breadcrumbs
1 onion, chopped
15 ml (1 tbsp) chopped parsley
15 ml (1 tbsp) brandy
Salt and freshly ground black pepper

Stock:
300 ml (½ pt · 1¼ cups) veal stock
150 ml (¼ pt · ⅔ cup) red wine
15 ml (1 tbsp) tomato purée (paste)
1 garlic clove, chopped
5 ml (1 tsp) yeast extract

1. Wash the heart then soak in water with a dash of vinegar for 30 minutes. Make an opening in the top and enlarge it for the stuffing.

2. Combine all the ingredients for the stuffing. Stuff the heart and fasten the opening with string.

3. Place in a casserole dish (Dutch oven) and brush with the melted butter or oil. Season then cook uncovered in the oven for 15 minutes at 200°C/400°F/gas mark 6. Add the stock, wine, tomato purée, garlic and yeast extract. Season again. Reduce the heat to 180°C/350°F/gas mark 4. Cover and braise for 45 minutes. Serve with carrots and peas.

 Beaujolais or rosé wine to accompany.

Preparation time: 15 minutes plus soaking.
Cooking time: 1 hour.

Tendons of Veal en Cocotte

The tendons of veal are the gristly portions found at the extremity of the breast of veal between the ribs. Cut into small portions, like spare ribs they make a delicious base for a casserole.

―∾ SERVES 4 ∾―

1 kg (2¼ lb) veal tendons or diced veal
50 g (2 oz · ½ cup) seasoned flour
15 ml (1 tbsp) curry powder
60 ml (4 tbsp) olive oil
15 ml (1 tbsp) tomato purée (paste)
600 ml (1 pt · 2½ cups) white wine
Sprig of thyme
1 celery stick, chopped
1 onion, chopped
2 garlic cloves, crushed
12 stoned (pitted) olives

1. Coat the tendons with the combined seasoned flour and curry powder.

2. Heat the oil in a large casserole (Dutch oven) and brown the meat for 10 minutes all over. Remove the surplus oil and add the remaining ingredients.

3. Cover with a lid and braise for 2 hours in the oven at 180°C/ 350°F/gas mark 4. Add water from time to time to keep the liquid level constant.

Garnish with new potatoes or cauliflower.

 Spanish red wine to accompany.

Preparation time: 15 minutes.
Cooking time: 2 hours.

Normandy-style Veal Cutlet Casserole

Veal cutlets are rather large portions which are best cooked in casserole dishes. Each cutlet should be 2.5 cm (1 in) thick, with the spinal bone removed (chined).

─── ∽ SERVES 2 ∽ ───

30 ml (2 tbsp) oil
2 veal cutlets
50 g (2 oz · ½ cup) seasoned flour

Normandy sauce:
2 apples, cored, peeled and cut in wedges
1 onion, chopped
1 celery stick, chopped
120 ml (4 fl oz · ½ cup) white wine
Salt and freshly ground black pepper
120 ml (4 fl oz · ½ cup) double (heavy) cream
5 ml (1 tsp) paprika

1. Heat the oil in a casserole (Dutch oven), dust the cutlets in the seasoned flour and brown for 5 minutes on each side. Remove the surplus oil and add the apple, onion, celery and white wine. Season then cover with a lid and braise in the oven for 45 minutes at 180°C/350°F/gas mark 4. Transfer meat to a warm serving plate.

2. Skim the gravy and blend in the cream. Season the sauce and pour over the cutlets. Sprinkle with paprika to finish.

Serve with braised chicory (endive) or French beans.

 Muscadet or Loire wine to accompany.

Preparation time: 20 minutes.
Cooking time: 45 minutes.

Osso Bucco

If you are serving rice with this dish, flavour it with saffron for an authentic Italian flavour.

∽ SERVES 6 ∾

60 ml (4 tbsp) oil
1.5 kg (3 lb) veal knuckles cut into 2.5 cm (1 in) thick rings
600 ml (1 pt · 2½ cups) water
300 ml (½ pt · 1¼ cups) white wine
Juice and grated rind of 1 lemon and 1 orange
5 ml (1 tsp) sugar
30 ml (2 tbsp) tomato purée (paste)
Salt and freshly ground black pepper
Sprig of thyme

Garnish:
2 carrots, diced
2 turnips, diced
2 celery sticks, diced
1 fennel bulb, sliced
2 garlic cloves, chopped
30 ml (2 tbsp) chopped parsley

1. In a large casserole (Dutch oven) heat the oil and brown the meat for 15 minutes. Add the water, wine, juice and grated rind of the lemon and orange, sugar and tomato purée. Cover with a lid and stew gently for 1½ hours.

2. Season to taste and add the thyme and vegetables. Cover with a lid and continue to cook for 45 minutes. Remove the meat and strain the sauce.

3. Serve the meat with the vegetables and sauce, sprinkle with the parsley before serving.

Serve with rice or pasta.

 Chianti Classico is the ideal accompaniment.

Preparation time: 30 minutes.
Cooking time: 2¼ hours.

73

~ **Chapter Five** ~

PORK AND BACON CASSEROLES

MODERN METHODS OF SELECTION AND feeding have resulted in a great improvement in the overall quality of British pork.

Pork and bacon make wonderfully flavoursome casseroles.

The best cuts of pork to use are neck end of loin, shoulder, knuckle, belly and hand. You can also buy ready diced 'casserole pork' in supermarkets.

Any joint of bacon is suitable for casseroling but pieces of collar and hock are cheaper than back or gammon. Most recipes recommend green (or unsmoked) joints, but use smoked if you prefer.

High-quality pork can be easily identified by its finely grained, firm but not flabby, flesh. The shoulder cuts in particular should be marbled with whiter fat, and the skin smooth and free from wrinkles. Bacon should be a good pink colour with white fat. The rind should be thin and elastic. Avoid any cuts which appear sticky or have a strong smell.

Because of the high fat content of pork and bacon, cooking the meat with acid fruits, particularly apples and fresh pineapple, helps to tenderise the meat as well as complement the flavour. It is also worth trimming the meat well before cooking.

Make sure you remove the maximum amount of surface fat as the cooking progresses too, so that the sauce or gravy will not be too greasy.

Boston Bean Belly Casserole

Serve this hearty meal with crusty bread and follow with a tossed green salad.

───────────────── ∽ SERVES 6 ∽ ─────────────────

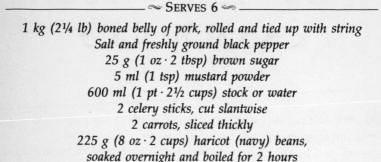

1 kg (2¼ lb) boned belly of pork, rolled and tied up with string
Salt and freshly ground black pepper
25 g (1 oz · 2 tbsp) brown sugar
5 ml (1 tsp) mustard powder
600 ml (1 pt · 2½ cups) stock or water
2 celery sticks, cut slantwise
2 carrots, sliced thickly
225 g (8 oz · 2 cups) haricot (navy) beans,
soaked overnight and boiled for 2 hours

1. Rub the belly with the salt, pepper, sugar and mustard.

2. Put the meat in a casserole dish (Dutch oven) with half the stock or water and celery. Cover and braise for 2 hours at 180°C/350°F/gas mark 4.

3. Add the carrots and the haricot beans and the remaining water or stock. Continue cooking for another 40 minutes. Uncover and cook for 10 more minutes to crisp the skin.

 Chablis or Hock to accompany.

Preparation time: 15 minutes plus soaking and cooking beans.
Cooking time: 3 hours.

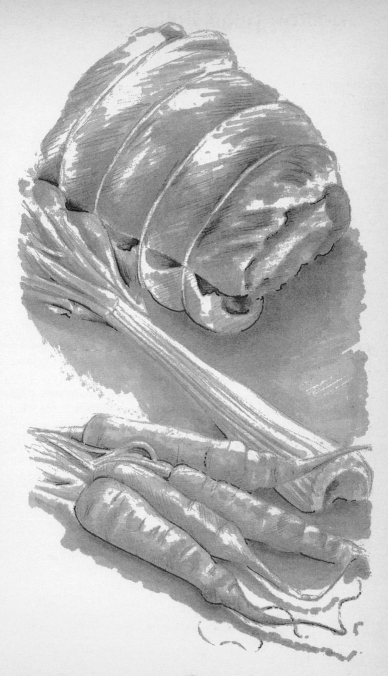

Pork with Apples

The tart apples and spices offset the richness of the pork beautifully.

*2.5 ml (½ tsp) each of cinnamon, mustard powder,
ground cloves, black pepper
5 ml (1 tsp) salt and 15 ml (1 tbsp) flour blended together
1 kg (2¼ lb) small loin of pork, rind and surplus fat removed*

Sauce:
*225 g (8 oz · 2 cups) onion, sliced
450 g (1 lb · 4 cups) apples, cored, peeled and sliced
300 ml (½ pt · 1¼ cups) sweet cider
1 stock cube*

1. Blend the spices and flour together and rub all over the meat.

2. Heat 30 ml (2 tbsp) oil in a casserole (Dutch oven) and brown the meat all over for 15 minutes.

3. Add the onion, apple, cider and stock cube. Cover with a lid and pot roast at 180°C/350°F/gas mark 4 for 2 hours. Baste with cider from time to time to keep the liquid level consistent.

 Muscadet or Chablis to accompany.

Preparation time: 25 minutes.
Cooking time: 2 hours.

Greek Cabbage Dolmas Casserole

Whether you use vine, spinach or cabbage leaves for dolmas this is a delicious dish. It can be eaten either hot or cold.

───────────── ∽ SERVES 4 ∽ ─────────────

8 green cabbage leaves
600 ml (1 pt · 2½ cups) water
4 slices of lemon
120 ml (4 fl oz · ½ cup) Greek yoghurt

Stuffing:
450 g (1 lb · 4 cups) good-quality sausagemeat
2 garlic cloves, chopped
1 egg
75 g (3 oz · ¾ cup) cooked rice
Salt and freshly ground black pepper

1. Blanch the cabbage leaves for 4 minutes. Refresh, drain and pat dry then spread on a chopping board.

2. In a casserole (Dutch oven) blend the sausagemeat with the garlic, egg, cooked rice and seasoning. Divide the mixture into 8 balls and place each one on a cabbage leaf and wrap the leaf around the stuffing.

3. Arrange the dolmas in the casserole dish. Cover with water then add the lemon slices. Cover and braise for 1 hour at 180°C/350°F/gas mark 4. Drain off 1 cup of the cooking liquid and mix it with the yoghurt in a bowl. Season to taste then pour over the dolmas and serve with jacket potatoes.

 White wine or wine cup to accompany.

Preparation time: 25 minutes.
Cooking time: 1 hour.

Pork Cutlets with Herbs

This dish is best cooked on one day, left to chill overnight and reheated and served the following day.

4 best end neck cutlets, each 225 g (8 oz · ½ lb),
trimmed of rind and fat
30 ml (2 tbsp) seasoned flour
30 ml (2 tbsp) oil
2 tomatoes, skinned, seeded and chopped
1 green chilli, seeded and chopped
300 ml (½ pt · 1¼ cups) dry white wine
60 ml (4 tbsp) chopped mixed herbs
(basil, parsley, garlic, chives, tarragon, spinach)

1. Coat the pork cutlets in the seasoned flour. Heat the oil in a casserole (Dutch oven). Fry (sauté) the cutlets for 4 minutes on each side then add the tomatoes, chilli, wine and herbs.

2. Cover with a lid and bake gently at 180°C/350°F/gas mark 4 for 1 hour. Add more wine during cooking to replace the liquid lost.

3. Cool if possible then chill overnight and reheat the next day.

Serve with noodles.

 German Hock to accompany.

Preparation time: 10 minutes.
Cooking time: 1 hour.

Bacon with Green Cabbage

A traditional Irish dish with lots of flavour.

1 kg (2¼ lb) piece of green lean back bacon, soaked overnight
if necessary
Water to cover
6 crushed peppercorns
1 green cabbage, cored and divided into quarters

1. Place the bacon in a casserole (Dutch oven) covered with cold water. Add the crushed peppercorns. Bring to the boil and simmer gently for 1½ hours. Add the green cabbage and cook for a further 30 minutes.

Serve with boiled new potatoes.

 Sparkling wine to accompany.

Preparation time: 5 minutes plus soaking if necessary.
Cooking time: 2 hours.

Polish-style Braised Gammon

Gammon can also be braised in dry cider, lager, dry white wine or simply water or fruit juices such as pineapple or orange.

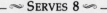

─────────────── ∾ SERVES 8 ∾ ───────────────

1 kg (2¼ lb) green gammon, soaked in water overnight
15 ml (1 tbsp) caraway seeds
30 ml (2 tbsp) brown sugar
750 ml (1¼ pt · 3 cups) sweet cider
1 onion, sliced
1 carrot, sliced
2 celery sticks, sliced

1. Place the gammon in a casserole (Dutch oven) with water and cook for 2 hours on a low heat. Drain and remove the skin from the meat.

2. Sprinkle over the caraway seeds and brown sugar then add the sweet cider, onion, carrot, and celery. Cover and braise for 30 minutes in a moderate oven at 180°C/350°F/gas mark 4. Cool in its own liquor and, when cold, serve with hot potato salad.

 Cider to accompany.

Preparation time: 5 minutes plus cooling time.
Cooking time: 2½ hours.

Dublin Sausage and Bacon Coddle

My late Irish wife, Mary, often produced this Dublin casserole which she improved with a garnish of sliced Black Pudding (blood sausage).

∽ SERVES 4 ∾

45 ml (3 tbsp) butter and 15 ml (1 tbsp) oil
8 fat pork sausages
8 thick green gammon slices
1 onion, sliced
4 potatoes, sliced
45 ml (3 tbsp) chopped parsley

Sauce:
300ml (½ pt · 1¼ cups) brown beer or stout
15 ml (1 tbsp) yeast extract
150 ml (¼ pt · ⅔ cup) water or beef stock
5 ml (1 tsp) salt
6 crushed black peppercorns
5 ml (1 tsp) made mustard

1. Heat the butter and oil in a large casserole (Dutch oven). Brown the sausages and gammon all over for 4 minutes. Add the onion and cook for a further 2 minutes. Remove the casserole from the heat and cover the meat with sliced potatoes.

2. In a bowl, combine the sauce ingredients and pour over the potatoes, sausages and gammon. Cover with a lid and braise for 45 minutes at 180°C/350°F/gas mark 4. When the potatoes are cooked the coddle is ready. Sprinkle on the parsley and serve.

 Stout to accompany.

Preparation time: 10 minutes.
Cooking time: 45 minutes.

Garlic Sausage and Cabbage Casserole

This tasty German recipe can be made quickly.

―――――――――――――― ∽ SERVES 4 ∽ ――――――――――――――

50 g (2 oz · ¼ cup) butter
225 g (8 oz · 2 cups) Savoy cabbage, finely shredded
1 onion, chopped
300 ml (½ pt · 1¼ cups) water
1 chicken stock cube
5 ml (1 tsp) caraway seeds
5 ml (1 tsp) salt and 6 crushed black peppercorns
30 ml (2 tbsp) gin
450 g (1 lb) garlic sausage, thickly sliced

1. In a casserole (Dutch oven) heat the butter and stir the cabbage and onion for 3 minutes to develop initial flavour. Add the water, stock cube, caraway seeds, salt, peppercorns and gin.

2. Cover with a lid and braise in the oven at 200°C/400°F/gas mark 6 for 20 minutes. Add the garlic sausage and heat for no more than 5 minutes with the lid on.

Serve with new boiled potatoes.

 Stout to accompany.

Preparation time: 10 minutes.
Cooking time: 25 minutes.

Chapter Six

LAMB CASSEROLES

THE PASSOVER PASCAL LAMB HAS BECOME a tradition. Its central part in the feasts to celebrate the Jewish festival or the Christian resurrection has made it an almost symbolic food. It is also a most versatile meat, happily combining with a whole variety of other flavours from herbs to spices, fruit to vegetables.

There are some 40 breeds of sheep in Britain. The term lamb refers to the flesh of a young animal, under one year's age and mutton refers to older animals. Age produces changes in the character of the flesh and bone and, to a certain degree, the nature of the fat deposited.

The most tender parts of the lamb are the best ends (cutlets), the loin and the legs, then come the shoulders, middle neck, scrag, and breast. For hot pot cookery, cuts from the middle neck and shoulders are usually the best pieces, provided the fat is removed before cooking.

Enamelled cast iron is regarded as one of the best materials for cookware. It enhances the flavour of any food cooked in it whether it be slow cooking in the oven or boiling, or frying on the hob. It also maintains a steadier heat which it holds for longer than other cookware materials.

Only use nylon pads to clean the pot and avoid harsh abrasive cleaners or wire pads. Do not heat over 230°C/450°F/gas mark 8 in the oven when using lids with plastic knobs and remember to use protective oven gloves when handling utensils which do not have insulated or wooden handles.

Lamb and Aubergine Casserole

This lamb dish, redolent of ratatouille, has been very popular in Mediterranean cuisine. It consists mainly of cheap cuts of lamb – middle neck or chump chops – with a base of aubergines sweet peppers and tomatoes.

―――――――――― ∞ SERVES 4 ∞ ――――――――――

30 ml (2 tbsp) oil
4 chump chops
1 aubergine (eggplant), peeled and sliced
1 green (bell) pepper, split, seeded and cut into small squares
1 tomato, skinned, seeded and chopped
1 onion, sliced
2 garlic cloves, crushed
Pinch of saffron
Salt and freshly ground black pepper
300 ml (½ pt · 1¼ cups) water or rosé wine

1. In a casserole (Dutch oven), heat the oil and brown the chops for 5 minutes. Add the aubergine, pepper, tomato, onion, garlic, saffron and seasoning.

2. Cover with water or wine and braise in the oven for 1¼ hours at 180°C/350°F/gas mark 4.

Serve with rice or pasta.

Provençal rosé to accompany.

Preparation time: 15 minutes.
Cooking time: 1¼ hours.

Lancashire Hot Pot

This is a traditional lamb dish from the north of England which is as old as King Arthur. Only potatoes and other white vegetables should be used, chump chops or pieces of neck.

―――――――――― ∽ SERVES 4–6 ∾ ――――――――――

30 ml (2 tbsp) oil
1 kg (2¼ lb) neck meat or chump chops
1 onion, sliced
2 parsnips, peeled and sliced
1 celery stick, sliced
450 g (1 lb) potatoes, sliced
1 l (1¾ pints · 4¼ cups) water
5 ml (1 tsp) salt
1 bouquet garni
1.25 ml (¼ tsp) coarsely ground black pepper

1. Pour the oil into the bottom of the casserole dish (Dutch oven) and layer the vegetables and meat alternately until three-quarters full. Top up with water and the bouquet garni. Add the salt and pepper then cover with lid and bake for 1¼ hours at 180°C/350°F/gas mark 4 on the middle shelf.

 English white wine to accompany.

Preparation time: 15 minutes.
Cooking time: 1¼ hours.

Braised Lamb Loaf
with Haricot Beans

This is an economical Latin American casserole, consisting of minced lamb bound with eggs and sweetcorn kernels.

~ SERVES 4 ~

60 ml (4 tbsp) corn oil
225 g (8 oz · 2 cups) minced (ground) lamb
1 egg, beaten
150 g (5 oz · 1¼ cups) cooked sweetcorn (corn) kernels
100 g (4 oz · 1 cup) cooked haricot (navy) beans
15 ml (1 tbsp) tomato purée (paste)
1 chilli, seeded and chopped
5 ml (1 tsp) salt
3 mint leaves, chopped
5 ml (1 tsp) desiccated (shredded) coconut

1. Pour the oil in a small casserole (Dutch oven). Combine all the ingredients in the casserole. Press down well.

2. Cover with a lid and braise for 1 hour at 180°C/350°F/gas mark 4.

When cooked leave to cool until completely cold. Then slice and serve with a tomato salad.

 Chilean wine to accompany.

Preparation time: 5 minutes plus cooling time.
Cooking time: 1 hour.

Lamb and Potato Casserole

You can purchase boned neck or breast of lamb very cheaply and it can be a very economical and tasty dish.

----------------- ∾ Serves 4 ∾ -----------------

45 ml (3 tbsp) olive oil
1 kg (2¼ lb) breast or neck of lamb, boned
4 rashers (slices) of streaky bacon,rindless and diced
8 button (pearl) onions
8 button mushrooms
450 g (1 lb · 4 cups) potatoes, cubed
150 ml (¼ pt · ⅔ cup) medium sherry
5 ml (1 tsp) Worcestershire sauce
300 ml (½ pt · 1¼ cups) water with 1 stock cube
Salt and freshly ground black pepper
5 ml (1 tsp) tomato purée (paste)

1. Heat the oil in a casserole (Dutch oven) and brown the meat for 6 minutes. Add the bacon, onions, mushrooms, potatoes, sherry, Worcestershire sauce and stock cube with water. Season to taste. Bring the liquid to the boil and add the tomato purée. Cover with a lid and bake in the oven at 180°C/350°F/gas mark 4 for 1½ hours.

Serve with cauliflower cheese and green vegetables.

Beaujolais Nouveau or Bulgarian Cabernet red wine to accompany.

Preparation time: 15 minutes.
Cooking time: 1½ hours.

Hunter's Lamb Casserole

This is a robust casserole with lots of flavour. Try it with red kidney beans instead of broad beans for a change.

—————————————— ∾ SERVES 6 ∾ ——————————————

60 ml (4 tbsp) oil
150 g (5 oz · 1¼ cups) onions, diced
1 red and 1 green (bell) peppers, seeded and cut into small cubes
2 garlic cloves, chopped
1 kg (2¼ lb) shoulder lamb, skinned and cubed
30 ml (2 tbsp) chopped tarragon
5 ml (1 tsp) crushed rosemary
150 g (5 oz · 2½ cups) button mushrooms, diced or quartered
15 g (½ oz · 2 tbsp) flour
150 ml (¼ pt · ⅔ cup) water
120 ml (4 fl oz · ½ cup) dry vermouth
Salt and freshly ground black pepper
150 g (5 oz · 1¼ cups) cooked broad (lima) beans,
canned, frozen, or fresh

1. Heat the oil in a casserole (Dutch oven) and stir-fry the onion until soft, not brown, for 1 minute. Add the garlic and peppers and stir-fry for a further minute.

2. Add the meat, herbs and mushrooms. Cook, stirring continuously until all the liquid has evaporated, for a further 5 minutes. Sprinkle with the flour and add the water, vermouth and seasoning.

3. Bake covered for 1 hour at 180°C/350°F/gas mark 4. When cooked, mix in the broad beans (skinned for a greener appearance).

Serve with rice or polenta.

 Beaujolais or Spanish red wine to accompany.

Preparation time: 25 minutes.
Cooking time: 1 hour.

Spanish-style Lamb

45 ml (3 tbsp) olive oil
1 kg (2¼ lb) lean shoulder lamb, boned and diced
450 g (1 lb · 4 cups) onions, diced
2 garlic cloves, chopped
Pinch of ground saffron
15 ml (1 tbsp) flour
450 g (1 lb · 4 cups) tomatoes, skinned, seeded, and chopped
5 ml (1 tsp) paprika
5 ml (1 tsp) ground cumin
2.5 ml (½ tsp) ground cloves
5 ml (1 tsp) freshly ground black pepper
1 l (1¾ pts · 4¼ cups) water and red wine, mixed
100 g (4 oz · 1 cup) butterfly pasta, cooked
45 ml (3 tbsp) chopped parsley

1. Heat the oil in a casserole (Dutch oven) and brown the meat
for 5 minutes. Add the onion, garlic and saffron and toss for 1
minute. Stir in the flour. Blend in the tomatoes, paprika and all the
spices. Finally, stir in the water and wine. Simmer for 1 hour in the
oven until the meat is tender at 180°C/350°F/gas mark 4. Check
and adjust the seasoning, add the pasta and serve sprinkled with
parsley.

 Rosé or Spanish red wine to accompany.

Preparation time: 20 minutes.
Cooking time: 1 hour.

Algerian Lamb and Pumpkin Casserole

Let me continue this selection of lamb dishes from around the world with a little-known but delicious African stew. Use about 450 g(1 lb) of pumpkin cubes; but you can vary this to suit your own taste.

----------- ∞ SERVES 6 ∞ -----------

1 kg (2¼ lb) lamb from shoulder,
cut into 2.5 cm (1 in) cubes, fat and bones removed
30 ml (2 tbsp) seasoned flour
60 ml (4 tbsp) oil
2 onions, chopped
3 garlic cloves, chopped
1 green chilli, seeded and chopped
2.5 cm (1 in) root ginger (ginger root), peeled and chopped
4 tomatoes, skinned, seeded and chopped
600 ml (1 pt · 2½ cups) water
1 pumpkin, skinned and cut into 2.5 cm (1 in) cubes
Salt and freshly ground black pepper

1. Dust the meat in flour and shake off any surplus. Heat the oil in a casserole (Dutch oven) and stir-fry the onions, garlic and chilli for 2 minutes. Add the ginger and meat and let it brown for 2 more minutes while tossing and stirring. Add the tomatoes, water, and pumpkin then cover the casserole and braise gently in oven for 1½ hours at 180°C/350°F/gas mark 4. Season at the last moment.

Serve with potatoes or rice.

 Algerian or Spanish red to accompany.

Preparation time: 20 minutes.
Cooking time: 1½ hours.

Lamb Cutlet and Potato Hot-pot

A quick and simple meal best served with a green vegetable.

_____ ❧ SERVES 4 ❧ _____

60 ml (4 tbsp) oil
8 lamb cutlets, trimmed and chined (boned)
450 g (1 lb · 4 cups) potatoes sliced
1 onion, sliced
300 ml (½ pt · 1¼ cups) water
1 stock cube
Salt and freshly ground black pepper
100 g (4 oz · 1 cup) Cheddar cheese, grated

1. Heat the oil in a flameproof casserole (Dutch oven) and brown the cutlets for just 1 minute on each side. Add the onion.

2. Cover with a layer of overlapping sliced potatoes.

3. Bring the water to the boil and stir in the stock cube until dissolved. Pour over the potatoes. Season to taste. Sprinkle over the grated cheese and bake at 200°C/400°F/gas mark 6 for 35 minutes.

 Cider or lager to accompany.

Preparation time: 15 minutes.
Cooking time: 35 minutes.

Braised Lamb Chops
with Aubergine Sauce

This is a special occasion casserole with a Mediterranean flavour.

―――――――――――――― ∾ SERVES 4 ∾ ――――――――――――――

8 small lamb chops, well trimmed of fat

Sauce:
5 ml (1 tsp) salt
1 aubergine (eggplant), diced
60 ml (4 tbsp) oil
50 g (2 oz · ½ cup) onion, chopped
2 garlic cloves, chopped
3 tomatoes, skinned, seeded and chopped
150 ml (¼ pt · ⅔ cup) red wine
Salt and freshly ground black pepper
5 ml (1 tsp) cornflour (cornstarch) and 45 ml (3 tbsp) water, mixed
350 g (12 oz · 1½ cups) Mozzarella cheese, diced
45 ml (3 tbsp) snipped chives

1. Sprinkle salt over the aubergine and leave for 30 minutes to help extract bitter juice then rinse in cold water and pat dry with kitchen paper.

2. Heat 30 ml (2 tbsp) of the oil in a casserole (Dutch oven) and cook the chops for 4 minutes on each side. Remove the chops and keep warm.

3. In the same pan heat the remaining oil and fry (sauté) the aubergine, onion and garlic, stirring and tossing evenly. Add the tomatoes, red wine and seasoning and cook, stirring for 10 minutes. Add the cornflour and water to make a thickish sauce. Return the chops. Sprinkle the cheese over the top and bake at 160°C/325°F/gas mark 3 for 30 minutes. Sprinkle over the chives just before serving.

 Macon or Beaujolais to accompany.

Preparation time: 25 minutes plus salting of aubergine.
Cooking time: 30 minutes.

Greek-style Fricassée of Lamb with Lemon

─── ⚬ SERVES 4–6 ⚬ ───

60 ml (4 tbsp) olive oil
White of 1 leek, sliced
1 kg (2¼ lb) shoulder lamb, cubed
15 ml (1 tbsp) flour
Salt and freshly ground black pepper
1 l (1¾ pts · 4¼ cups) water
1 fennel bulb, sliced
15 ml (1 tbsp) cornflour (cornstarch)
3 egg yolks
Juice and grated rind of 1 lemon
90 ml (6 tbsp) water
30 ml (2 tbsp) chopped lemon grass or parsley

1. Heat the oil in a casserole (Dutch oven) and stir-fry the leek for 1 minute. Add the lamb and fry (sauté) for 4 minutes without browning. Stir in the flour. Season with salt and pepper. Add the water and fennel and bring to the boil. Gently simmer for 1½ hours.

2. Whisk together the cornflour, egg yolks, lemon juice and rind and water and gradually add a ladleful of the meat stock. Stir the egg mixture into the stew. Taste and adjust seasoning.

On serving, sprinkle with lemon grass or parsley. Serve with new potatoes or rice.

 Domestica or other Greek wine to accompany.

Preparation time: 25 minutes.
Cooking time: 1½ hours.

Spanish-style Lamb Chops

In 1492 the Conils enlisted in the Spanish army to repel the invasion of the Arabs. As a reward they were given a vast territory of land south of Cadiz. The town still exists under the family name. Here is a dish to remind us of this event.

─────────────── ∼ SERVES 6 ∽ ───────────────

60 ml (4 tbsp) olive oil
450 g (1 lb · 4 cups) potatoes, sliced
450 g (1 lb · 4 cups) onions, sliced
450 g (1 lb · 4 cups) tomatoes, skinned, seeded and chopped
6 lamb shoulder chops
2 green (bell) peppers, seeded and chopped
1 head of garlic, cloves separated and roasted
Pinch of ground saffron
Pinch each of ground cinnamon, cloves, and mace
Salt and freshly ground black pepper
600 ml (1 pt · 2½ cups) Spanish white wine or pale sherry

1. Put the oil in a casserole (Dutch oven) and add alternate layers of potatoes, onions, and tomatoes. Place the meat on top.
2. Add the green peppers, roasted garlic, the spices and the wine. Cover and bake in a hot oven 200°C/400°F/gas mark 6 for 20 minutes then reduce the heat to 180°C/350°F/gas mark 4 and cook for a further 2 hours.

Serve with a side salad.

 Muscadet or rosé wine to accompany.

Preparation time: 20 minutes.
Cooking time: 2 hours 20 minutes.

Irish Stew

The presentation is improved by reserving a few whole potatoes to cook and serve as a garnish as the ones in the stew tend to 'fall' to thicken the gravy.

─────────────── ∽ SERVES 6 ∽ ───────────────

225 g (8 oz · 2 cups) onions, sliced
750 g (1½ lb · 6 cups) potatoes, sliced
1 kg (2¼ lb) shoulder of lamb, skin and fat removed,
cut into 2.5 cm (1 in) cubes or middle neck cutlets
1 stock cube dissolved in
600 ml (1 pt · 2½ cups) water
5 ml (1 tsp) salt
1.5 ml (¼ tsp) white pepper
Sprig of thyme
30 ml (2 tbsp) chopped parsley

1. Place the vegetables and lamb in layers in the casserole: onions, potato, lamb, finishing with potatoes. Pour over the stock, season and add the sprig of thyme. Cover and braise gently for 2 hours in a low oven at 180°C/350°F/gas mark 4.

Sprinkle over the parsley just before serving in soup plates.

 Stout or lager to accompany.

Preparation time: 15 minutes.
Cooking time: 2 hours.

Italian-style Lamb Stew

This casserole contains chilli which many claim prevents or cures a number of different ailments with its fiery taste. This dish can also be prepared with cooked lamb, thus saving time, but the flavour is not as delicate. The chilli can be replaced by mild red and green (bell) peppers if desired.

~ SERVES 4–6 ~

225g (8 oz · ½ lb) Fettucine pasta
1 kg (2¼ lb) small leg of lamb, boned
60 ml (4 tbsp) olive or cooking oil
225 g (8 oz · ½ lb) back bacon, cut in thin strips
1 green and 1 red chilli, seeded and cut in thin strips
2 garlic cloves, chopped
150 g (5 oz · 1¼ cups) onions, cut in thin strips (julienne)
300 ml (½ pt · 1¼ cups) water and white wine mixed
300 ml (½ pt · 1¼ cups) double (heavy) cream
Salt and freshly ground black pepper
150 g (5 oz · 1¼ cups) Parmesan or any hard cheese, grated
30 ml (2 tbsp) chopped basil and parsley

1. Boil the fettucine in a casserole (Dutch oven) for 8 minutes. Drain and rinse in hot water. Drain again and keep hot.

2. Slice the lamb and cut it into thin strips the same thickness as the fettucine.

3. In a casserole, heat the oil and stir-fry the lamb and bacon with the chilli and garlic for 3 minutes without browning. Add the onion and cook until dry for another 4 minutes, tossing and stirring all the time. Pour in the water and wine and cook in the oven for 45 minutes at 180°C/350°F/gas mark 4. Add the fettucine and the cream. Season to taste.

Sprinkle over the grated cheese and herbs before serving.

 Chianti to accompany.

Preparation time: 30 minutes.
Cooking time: 45 minutes.

Lamb Stew with Haricot Beans

This dish is traditionally made with mutton, but lamb is fine. Use a drained can of haricot beans for quickness.

─────────────── ∾ SERVES 8 ∾ ───────────────

150 g (5 oz · 1¼ cups) haricot (navy) beans,
soaked overnight and boiled for 2 hours
45 ml (3 tbsp) oil
1 kg (2¼ lb) shoulder lamb, cut in cubes
30 ml (2 tbsp) flour
100 g (4 oz · 1 cup) rindless streaky bacon, diced
150 g (5 oz · 1¼ cups) onions, chopped
2 garlic cloves, chopped
150 g (5 oz · 1¼ cups) carrots, diced
150 g (5 oz · 1¼ cups) celery, sliced
60 ml (4 tbsp) tomato purée (paste)
5 ml (1 tsp) sugar
5 ml (1 tsp) salt
1.5 ml (¼ tsp) freshly ground black pepper
1 l (1¾ pts · 4¼ cups) water

1. Heat the oil in a casserole (Dutch oven) and brown the lamb and bacon for 5 minutes. Sprinkle over the flour and add the onion, garlic, other ingredients and water. Bring to the boil and gently braise in the oven for 45 minutes at 180°C/350°F/gas mark 4. Add the beans and cook for a further 45 minutes or until the meat and beans are tender. Season to taste.

Stout or cider to accompany.

Preparation time: 25 minutes.
Cooking time: 1½ hours.

Lamb and Apricot Casserole

For quickness, use ready-to-eat dried apricots. But for the best flavour of all, soak the apricots in freshly brewed tea instead of water.

_____ ∼ SERVES 4 ∼ _____

30 ml (2 tbsp) oil
1 kg (2¼ lb) half a shoulder of lamb
450 g (1 lb · 2⅔ cups) dried apricots, soaked for 6 hours in water
300 ml (½ pt · 1¼ cups) water or orange juice
Salt and freshly ground black pepper
4 ml (¾ tsp) ground cumin
30 ml (2 tbsp) clear honey
1 green chilli, seeded and sliced
30 ml (2 tbsp) clear honey

1. Heat the oil in a casserole (Dutch oven) and sear the meat for 8 minutes until brown all over. Add the apricots, water or orange juice, salt and pepper, ground cumin and green chilli.

2. Transfer to the oven and bake at 200°C/400°F/gas mark 6 for 40 minutes. Add the honey and cook for 10 more minutes. Serve with mangetout (snow peas) or French beans.

Muscadet or Chablis to accompany.

Preparation time: 10 minutes plus soaking time.
Cooking time: 50 minutes.

Rack of Lamb with Mushrooms

The best end of lamb is always a popular dish when pot roasted. Some people prefer lamb under done, others well done, so adjust the time of cooking according to taste. Most chefs cook rack of lamb for 30 minutes; cook it for 45 minutes if you like it well done.

― ❦ SERVES 4 ❧ ―

45 ml (3 tbsp) butter and oil combined
1 rack of lamb, trimmed and chined (spinal bones removed)
120 ml (4 fl oz · ½ cup) medium Sherry
120 ml (4 fl oz · ½ cup) water or meat stock
5 ml (1 tsp) tomato purée (paste)
Salt and freshly ground black pepper
450 g (1 lb) field or wild mushrooms

1. Heat the oil in a flameproof casserole (Dutch oven) and brown the rack of lamb for 8 minutes, then transfer into the oven without a lid. Cook for 25 minutes at 200°C/400°F/gas mark 6.

2. Remove the surplus fat from the casserole then add the sherry, water, tomato purée, seasoning and cleaned mushrooms. Cover with a lid and cook for 10–20 minutes.

Cut the rack into cutlets and serve with sautéed potatoes and broccoli.

Red Australian Cabernet to accompany.

Preparation time: 20 minutes.
Cooking time: 45 minutes.

Casseroled Lamb Dumplings in Saffron Rice

An unusual casserole with a Middle-Eastern flavour.

∼ SERVES 6 ∼

450 g (1 lb · 4 cups) lean minced (ground) lamb
45 ml (3 tbsp) chopped mixed herbs: parsley, mint, and basil
30 ml (2 tbsp) breadcrumbs
2 eggs, beaten
50 g (2 oz · ⅓ cup) raisins
1 green chilli, seeded and chopped (optional)
Salt and freshly ground black pepper
2 onions, chopped
90 ml (6 tbsp) oil
150 g (5 oz · ⅔ cup) long-grain rice
Pinch of ground saffron
1 garlic clove, chopped
450 ml (¾ pt · 2 cups) water
Salt and freshly ground black pepper

1. For the dumplings, in a casserole (Dutch oven) combine the minced lamb, herbs, breadcrumbs, eggs, raisins, chilli (if using), seasoning and half the onion. Divide into 16 small dumplings. Put on one side. Heat half the oil in the casserole and brown the dumplings for 5 minutes. Remove and set aside.

2. For the rice, heat the remaining oil in the casserole and stir-fry the remaining onion until golden. Add the rice, saffron, garlic and water and bring to the boil for 8 minutes. Season. Add the dumplings. Cover and bake for 25–30 minutes at 200°C/400°F/gas mark 6.

 Rosé wine to accompany.

Preparation time: 25 minutes.
Cooking time: 25–30 minutes.

Chapter Seven

POULTRY CASSEROLES

ALL TYPES OF POULTRY, WHETHER DOMESTICATED or wild, can be cooked in similar ways. A classic Coq au Vin, for instance, could be produced with pheasant, guinea-fowl, turkey and even with duck, although it would be more fatty.

There are two types of chicken casserole dishes: the pot roasted casserole which the chefs call *poëllé* using the whole bird cooked in an oval casserole fitting the size of the bird. The second style is classically referred to as *oven sauteed,* where the raw portions of poultry are cooked in the oven with enough liquid to provide a good sauce. Both styles are cooked with the lid on. The lid is only removed to brown the bird.

There is also a difference between brown and white sauce casseroles. For the latter, cream is added and the chicken is cooked without colouring the skin, whereas in brown sauces, the skin is coloured before braising. The flavour of the birds emanates from the fatty skin. Hence the crucial importance of not discarding it before cooking.

About Poultry

Generally speaking, the term 'poultry' is applied to all domesticated birds that have been bred and fattened for the table. These include ducks, geese, turkeys, guinea fowl, as well as domestic pigeon and quail reared on farms.

Fowl Family

Fowl are graded according to age and how they were fed:

(a) Squab chickens (poussins) 10–12 weeks old and weighing 500 g/1 lb per portion.

(b) Spring chickens or poulet nouveau, 12–16 weeks, weighing 750 g/1½ lb for two portions.

(c) Broilers or poulet de grain, weighing 1 kg/2 lb for two portions.

(d) Roasters or poulet reine, weighing 1.5 kg/3 lb for four portions.

(e) Capons, young castrated males, weighing 3 kg/7 lb for six portions.

(f) Poularde, castrated females, weighing 3 kg/7 lb for six portions.

(g) Old hens or cocks for boiling, over two years old, for six portions (mostly used for pie meat and not available in supermarkets but only direct from farmers).

Signs of Quality

Chickens are divided into two categories according to what they were fed:

(a) milk fed

(b) corn or maize fed, which have yellow flesh

A young chicken should have tender flesh which is elastic to the touch, but not flabby. The breast bone should be soft and flexible and should have a well rounded breast, fleshy thighs, and well distributed fat. The claws may be white or black, according to the species, but they should never be yellow. They should be soft and pliable.

Casseroled Turkey Patties
with Chestnuts

You can cook and shell your own chestnuts or use canned or frozen.

─────────── ∾ SERVES 4 ∾ ───────────

Patties:
225 g (8 oz · 2 cups) minced (ground) turkey
150 g (5 oz · 1¼ cups) pork sausagemeat
1 egg, beaten
100 g (4 oz · 1 cup) cooked chestnuts
15 ml (1 tbsp) chopped parsley
1 onion, chopped
5 ml (1 tsp) whisky
Salt and freshly ground black pepper
50 g (2 oz · ¼ cup) butter and 30 ml (2 tbsp) oil for cooking

Sauce:
150 ml (¼ pt · ⅔ cup) ginger wine
50 g (2 oz · ¼ cup) sugar
2 tsp cornflour (cornstarch) and 30 ml (2 tbsp) water, mixed
225 g (8 oz · 2 cups) cranberries

1. Combine all the ingredients for the patties except the butter and oil. Divide into four large balls. Flatten and coat with seasoned flour. Shape them like fish cakes.

2. Heat the butter and oil in a shallow casserole (Dutch oven). Brown the patties for 4 minutes on each side. Pour off fat.

3. Liquidise the sauce ingredients and pour over. Cover and bake for 15 minutes at 200°C/400°F/gas mark 6. Stir in the cranberries. Season to taste. Serve with sprouts.

 Rosé or Muscadet to accompany.

Preparation time: 20 minutes.
Cooking time: 15 minutes.

Basque-style Chicken Casserole

A rustic-style dish from Northern Spain.

8 chicken portions
45 ml (3 tbsp) seasoned flour
60 ml (4 tbsp) olive oil

1 red, 1 green and 1 yellow (bell) pepper, seeded and sliced
1 Spanish onion, sliced
3 garlic cloves, chopped
300 ml (½ pt · 1¼ cups) dry white wine
4 cup mushrooms, sliced
3 tomatoes, skinned, seeded and chopped
45 ml (3 tbsp) chopped parsley

5 ml (1 tsp) salt
5 ml (1 tsp) freshly ground black pepper
150 ml (¼ pt · ⅔ cup) white wine
100 ml (3½ fl oz · 6½ tbsp) water
1 chicken stock cube, crumbled

1. Coat the chicken with the seasoned flour and shake off any surplus.

2. Heat the oil in a flameproof casserole (Dutch oven) and brown the chicken pieces for 10 minutes. Add the peppers, onion, garlic, wine and mushrooms. Cover and braise in the oven at 200°C/400°F/gas mark 6 for 15 minutes.

3. Stir all the remaining ingredients into the mixture. Replace the lid and cook for a further 10 minutes or until the chicken is cooked through.

The best accompaniment for this dish is rice.

 Spanish white wine to accompany.

Preparation time: 15 minutes.
Cooking time: 35 minutes.

Turkey Casserole with Tarragon

This simple dish of turkey cooked in its own stock without colouring is a great favourite with many people.

───────── ∽ SERVES 4 ∽ ─────────

1 breast of turkey, 750 g (1½ lb), cut into 50 g (2 oz · ⅛ lb) pieces
300 ml (½ pt · 1¼ cups) water
300 ml (½ pt · 1¼ cups) dry white wine
1 chicken stock cube
30 ml (2 tbsp) coarsely chopped tarragon
150 g (5 oz · ⅓ lb) baby carrots, trimmed and cleaned
150 g (5 oz · ⅓ lb) white turnips, cut into wedges
2 celery sticks, cut into fingers
4 small leeks, white part only
8 mangetout (snow peas)
4 spring onions (scallions)
Sprig of thyme
5 ml (1 tsp) salt and 6 crushed peppercorns

1. Put all the ingredients in a casserole (Dutch oven). Season with salt and crushed peppercorns. Cook, covered, in the oven for 1 hour at 200°C/400°F/gas mark 6.

Serve with new potatoes.

 Hock or Moselle to accompany.

Preparation time: 20 minutes.
Cooking time: 1 hour.

Cockie Leekie Casserole

This is another simple chicken dish I used to produce at the Arts Club.

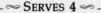

4 chicken breasts
30 ml (2 tbsp) seasoned flour
50 g (2 oz · ¼ cup) butter
4 small slices of green gammon, rindless
8 small leeks, white parts only
5 ml (1 tsp) salt
5 ml (1 tsp) freshly ground black pepper
300 ml (½ pt · 1¼ cups) medium sherry
1 chicken stock cube, crumbled in
150 ml (¼ pt · ⅔ cup) water

1. Coat the chicken breasts with seasoned flour and shake off the surplus.

2. Heat the butter in a casserole (Dutch oven) and fry (sauté) the chicken quickly to develop flavour but do not brown.

3. Remove from the casserole, then layer the chicken, gammon and leeks in the casserole. Season and add sherry and stock. Cover and braise in the oven at 180°C/350°F/gas mark 4 for 1½ hours.

 Muscadet or Chablis to accompany.

Preparation time: 20 minutes.
Cooking time: 1½ hours.

Channel Islands Chicken

This chicken dish which uses Jersey cream is comparable to, if not better than, the famous *Poulet Normande*.

4 chicken breasts
30 ml (2 tbsp) seasoned flour
50 g (2 oz · ¼ cup) butter and 15 ml (1 tbsp) oil combined
8 button mushrooms
8 button (pearl) onions, peeled
5 ml (1 tsp) salt
5 ml (1 tsp) white pepper
Pinch of dried thyme
2.5 ml (½ tsp) grated nutmeg
150 ml (¼ pt · ⅔ cup) medium white vermouth
150 ml (¼ pt · ⅔ cup) thick double (heavy) cream

1. Coat the chicken pieces with seasoned flour and shake off surplus.

2. Heat the butter and oil in a casserole (Dutch oven) and fry (sauté) the chicken pieces to develop flavour but do not brown. Add the mushrooms and onions. Cook for 2 minutes. Then blend in the remaining ingredients except for the cream. Cover and cook at 180°C/350°F/gas mark 4 for 1 hour. Just before serving stir the cream into the chicken gravy. Check the seasoning and serve with new Jersey potatoes.

 Hock or an Alsace wine to accompany.

Preparation time: 10 minutes.
Cooking time: 1 hour.

Coq au Vin with Port

This celebrated chicken dish is very succulent since all the gravy soaks into the chicken meat. The better the wine used the better the taste of the finished dish.

I prefer to use ruby port. But if you wish to use red wine, I suggest you choose a good Burgundy. I like a Côte de Beaune-Villages.

∽ SERVES 4 ∽

4 chicken legs, separated into drumsticks and thighs
10 ml (2 tsp) seasoned flour
60 ml (4 tbsp) oil
2 back bacon rashers (slices), rindless and diced
8 button (pearl) onions, peeled
8 button mushrooms
300 ml (½ pt · 1¼ cups) ruby port
150 ml (¼ pt · ⅔ cup) water
5 ml (1 tsp) yeast extract
2.5 ml (½ tsp) mixed ground spices
2 garlic cloves, crushed and chopped
15 ml (1 tbsp) tomato purée (paste)
5 ml (1 tsp) dried thyme
30 ml (2 tbsp) mixture of chopped parsley and tarragon

1. Coat the chicken pieces with seasoned flour and shake off the surplus.

2. Heat the oil in a flameproof casserole (Dutch oven) and the brown chicken pieces and bacon together for 5 minutes. Add the onions after 3 minutes and when slightly golden add the mushrooms.

3. Blend in all the remaining ingredients, except the herbs. Cover with a lid and braise gently for 1 hour at 180°C/350°F/gas mark 4. Sprinkle with the herbs just before serving.

Serve with noodles or shell pasta.

 Chablis or Rosé wine to accompany.

Preparation time: 20 minutes.
Cooking time: 1 hour.

Portuguese-style Chicken Casserole

Here is another favourite classic chicken dish, this time with tomatoes and onions.

─────────── ∽ SERVES 4 ∾ ───────────

4 breasts of chicken, cut into halves
30 ml (2 tbsp) seasoned flour
5 ml (1 tsp) paprika
60 ml (4 tbsp) olive oil
1 Spanish onion, chopped
4 tomatoes, skinned, seeded and chopped
15 ml (1 tbsp) tomato purée (paste)
150 ml (¼ pt · ⅔ cup) white Spanish wine
100 ml (3½ fl oz · 6½ tbsp) water
8 stuffed Spanish olives
5 ml (1 tsp) salt
5 ml (1 tsp) freshly ground black pepper
1 chicken stock cube, crumbled
1 garlic clove, crushed
Pinch of saffron
30 ml (2 tbsp) chopped coriander (cilantro)

1. Coat the chicken pieces with the seasoned flour and paprika combined and shake off any surplus.

2. Heat the oil in a casserole (Dutch oven), brown the chicken pieces for 8 minutes. Add the onion and cook for 2 more minutes, stirring well.

3. Stir in all the remaining ingredients except the coriander. Cover and braise in the oven for 1½ hours at 180°C/350°F/gas mark 4.

4. Sprinkle on the chopped coriander and serve with rice.

 Chablis or Spanish rosé to accompany.

Preparation time: 15 minutes.
Cooking time: 1½ hours.

Duck with Chick Peas

This casserole of duck with chick peas has been popular in Algeria for many years. It is extremely nourishing and tasty.

———————— ∾ SERVES 4 ∾ ————————

1.75 kg (4 lb) duck, cut into 8 portions
30 ml (2 tbsp) seasoned flour
60 ml (4 tbsp) oil
300 ml (½ pt · 1¼ cups) orange juice
150 ml (¼ pt · ⅔ cup) pomegranate juice (Grenadine)
15 ml (1 tbsp) yeast extract
300 ml (½ pt · 1¼ cups) duck stock or water
5 ml (1 tsp) salt
Pinch of chilli powder
Pinch of ground cumin
2 garlic cloves, chopped
1 onion, chopped

Garnish:
225 g (8 oz · 1⅓ cups) cooked chick peas (garbanzos)
(canned may be more convenient)
1 fennel bulb, sliced thinly

1. Coat the duck pieces in seasoned flour. Shake off the surplus.

2. Heat the oil in a casserole dish (Dutch oven) and brown the duck all over for 5 minutes.

3. Stir in the remaining ingredients. Braise in the oven covered with a lid for 45 minutes at 190°C/375°F/gas mark 5. Remove the surplus fat then add the chick peas and fennel and cook for another 45 minutes at 160°C/325°F/gas mark 3. Again skim off fat. Serve with couscous or rice.

 Algerian wine to accompany.

Preparation time: 10 minutes.
Cooking time: 1½ hours.

Casserole of Farm-Fed Pigeons

Pigeon is a delicacy by any standard, especially if well fed and domesticated. Young birds are tender and, like grouse, should not be overcooked but older birds need long simmering in a casserole.

————————— ∾ SERVES 4 ∾ —————————

4 pigeons, cut in halves
30 ml (2 tbsp) seasoned flour
45 ml (3 tbsp) oil
5 ml (1 tsp) salt
2.5 ml (½ tsp) freshly ground black pepper
600 ml (1 pt · 2½ cups) brown beer
15 ml (1 tbsp) yeast extract
Juice of 1 lemon
15 ml (1 tbsp) brown sugar
5 ml (1 tsp) tomato purée (paste)

Garnish:
225 g (8 oz · 2 cups) cooked fresh or frozen peas
8 cooked spring onions (scallions)

1. Coat the pigeons with seasoned flour and shake off any surplus.
2. Heat the oil in a flameproof casserole (Dutch oven) and brown the pigeon pieces all over for 10 minutes.
3. Stir in all the remaining ingredients. Cover with a lid and braise for 1½ hours over a low heat or in the oven at 160°C/325°F/gas mark 3 until meat detaches itself from the bone.
4. Add the cooked garnish to the pigeons. Check the seasoning and serve.

 Rosé wine or cider to accompany.

Preparation time: 15 minutes.
Cooking time: 1½ hours.

Barcelona-style Sautéd Chicken

This dish is made with boned and skinned chicken, which can be purchased in supermarkets. Just cut the breast and leg into 2.5 cm (1 in) pieces.

～ SERVES 4 ～
---

90 ml (6 tbsp) oil
2 rashers (slices) streaky bacon, rinded and diced
450 g (1 lb · 4 cups) chicken pieces
1 red onion, chopped
1 green chilli, deseeded and chopped
4 garlic cloves, chopped
45 ml (3 tbsp) seasoned flour
300 ml (½ pt · 1¼ cups) white Spanish wine
6 tomatoes, skinned, seeded and chopped
1 celery stick, chopped
Pinch of saffron
Salt and freshly ground black pepper
6 basil leaves, chopped

1. In a casserole (Dutch oven) heat the oil. Brown the bacon and chicken for 15 minutes. Add the onion, chilli and garlic. Cook for 30 seconds while stirring.

2. Sprinkle in the seasoned flour to absorb the surplus oil. Blend in the white wine and boil for 4 minutes. Stir in the tomatoes.

3. Add the celery, saffron and seasoning. Cover with a lid and braise in the oven for 35–40 minutes at 180°C/350°F/gas mark 4.

Sprinkle with the chopped basil leaves and serve with plain rice or fresh noodles.

 Spanish wine to accompany.

Preparation time: 30 minutes.
Cooking time: 35–40 minutes.

Farmhouse Chicken Casserole

This casserole is equally good made with small turkey breasts.

———————————— ∽ SERVES 4 ∽ ————————————

60 ml (4 tbsp) butter and oil combined
100 g (4 oz · ½ cup) lean bacon rashers (slices), rinded and diced
2 carrots, peeled and diced
1 onion, chopped
the white of two leeks, sliced, washed and drained
1 celery stick, sliced
4 chicken breasts, 225 g (8 oz · ½ lb) each, bone and skin removed
400 ml (14 fl oz · 1¾ cups) water mixed with 2 chicken stock cubes
Sprig of thyme
225 g (8 oz) white mushrooms, quartered
Juice and grated rind of 1 lemon
8 small potatoes, each the size of an egg
Salt and freshly ground black pepper
1 egg yolk
120 ml (4 fl oz · ½ cup) double (heavy) cream
5 ml (1 tsp) cornflour (cornstarch)
Grated nutmeg

1. In a casserole (Dutch oven), heat the butter and oil and stir-fry the bacon and vegetables for 5 minutes, then add the chicken and toss for 3 minutes.

2. Add the water and stock cubes, thyme, mushrooms, lemon and potatoes. Season and cook gently for 25 minutes.

3. In a bowl blend together the egg yolk, cream, cornflour and nutmeg and add 120 ml (4 fl oz · ½ cup) of the cooking juices. Blend this mixture into the rest of the gravy, heat through but do not boil. Season to taste.

 Rosé, Muscadet or Chablis to accompany.

Preparation time: 25 minutes.
Cooking time: 30 minutes.

Chicken Curry with Pineapple

This is a very tasty oriental chicken dish cooked with coconut milk and spices.

―――――――――――――― ∽ SERVES 4 ∾ ――――――――――――――

4 boned legs and 2 breasts of chicken, boned and diced
75 ml (5 tbsp) oil
1 onion, chopped
1 garlic clove, chopped
450 ml (¾ pt · 2 cups) water
Juice and grated rind of 1 lemon
30 ml (2 tbsp) honey
7.5 ml (½ tbsp) tomato purée (paste)
2.5 ml (½ tsp) salt
100 g (4 oz · ½ cup) pineapple, fresh or canned, in cubes

Curry powder mixture:
30 ml (2 tbsp) desiccated (shredded) coconut, lightly toasted
30 ml (2 tbsp) curry powder
1.5 ml (¼ tsp) ground cinnamon
5 ml (1 tsp) ground ginger

1. Mix together all the curry powder ingredients and rub over the chicken pieces. Shake off any surplus.

2. In a casserole (Dutch oven) heat the oil and fry (sauté) the chicken pieces for 5 minutes on each side. Turn frequently. Add the onion and garlic and cook for 1 minute. Pour in the water, lemon rind, juice, honey and tomato purée. Season and bake gently for 45 minutes, covered, at 180°C/350°F/gas mark 4. Five minutes before it is ready, add the pineapple cubes.

Heat through and serve with plain boiled rice.

 Chilled fruit juices to accompany.

Preparation time: 15 minutes.
Cooking time: 45 minutes.

Chicken Casserole with Beaujolais Nouveau

The classic garnish of glazed onions and mushrooms is cooked separately. Simply omit if you don't want to use another pan!

---— ∞ SERVES 4 ∞ ———---

1.5 kg (3 lb) chicken, cut into 8 pieces
45 ml (3 tbsp) seasoned flour
100 g (4 oz · ½ cup) mixed oil and butter
1 onion, chopped
1 carrot, diced
600 ml (1 pt · 2½ cups) Beaujolais Nouveau
1 chicken stock cube
Sprig of thyme
2 garlic cloves, chopped
15 ml (1 tbsp) tomato purée (paste)
5 ml (1 tsp) sugar
Salt and freshly ground black pepper
2.5 ml (½ tsp) ground mace
30 ml (2 tbsp) chopped parsley
1.5 ml (¼ tsp) mixed spice

Garnish:
12 button onions
12 button mushrooms
5 ml (1 tsp) cornflour, 45 ml (3 tbsp) water, 5 ml (1 tsp) yeast extract combined

1. Rub the chicken pieces in seasoned flour and shake off the surplus.

2. Reserve 30 ml (2 tbsp) of butter. Heat the oil and remaining butter in a casserole (Dutch oven) and brown the chicken for 15 minutes. Add the chopped onion and carrot and toss for 2 minutes. Pour in the wine and boil for 5 minutes.

3. Add the stock cube, sprig of thyme, garlic and tomato purée and boil 4 minutes. Season and simmer in the oven for 45 minutes at 180°C/350°F/gas mark 4.

4. While the chicken is cooking, boil the onions for 4 minutes and the mushrooms for 30 seconds. Drain. Heat 30 ml (2 tbsp) butter in a pan with 5 ml (1 tsp) of sugar until it becomes sticky. Toss the onions and mushrooms in this butterscotch mixture to glaze for 2 minutes. Season with salt, pepper, mace and a pinch of mixed spice and serve as a garnish.

5. When the chicken is cooked, stir together the cornflour, water and yeast extract and add to the casserole. Boil for 4 minutes to clear the starch.

Sprinkle with the parsley on serving. This dish tastes even more delicious cold with salad as the sauce has a jellied texture.

 Beaujolais to accompany.

Preparation time: 30 minutes.
Cooking time: 45 minutes.

Chapter Eight

VEGETABLE CASSEROLES

IF YOU ARE MAKING A REALLY DETERMINED effort to persuade your family or friends to eat more vegetables, you will find that they will respond more readily if the vegetables are appealing, not overcooked, crisp, crunchy and fresh looking. Think of the irresistible charm of vegetables floating like flowers in a Japanese lacquered pool. The French have created many solo vegetable entrées for the same purpose. There was a time when the Great French King Louis XIV elevated mangetout (snow peas) to a delicacy to be eaten on their own. The people of India consider vegetable dishes as almost sacrosanct. Gourmet vegetarian dishes were created in that continent where a thousand fragrances can be captured in a single dish of lentils. They do not boil spinach, but stir fry it in clarified butter. They understand how to balance pulses with starchy vegetables for a better diet. They know how to cook vegetables.

Unfortunately, 'à l'Anglaise' was often interpreted in our master chef culinary circles as a great joke. If you can't cook you can always boil cabbage until doomsday. And cabbage soup has been served in many prisons and concentration camps as the only food. The Germans made better use of cabbages by fermenting them as sauerkraut for preservation. In many countries dry vegetables have been the staple diet: beans, peas, peanuts and dry lentils.

Badly cooked vegetables seem to be a general complaint. However, this has been remedied in recent years by a younger generation of chefs who launched Nouvelle Cuisine with the art of embellishing their meat dishes with beautifully carved and underdone vegetables.

Fresh vegetables must be really fresh, because the fresher and crisper they are the higher the vitamin content. But are we so short of these vitamins from vegetables that we could not manage without them? The answer is to be found in basic nutrition books. The myth about spinach has now been dispelled. There is more iron in liver than in spinach; more Vitamin C in fresh citrus fruit juice than in new potatoes boiled in the skin. Vitamin A is found in orange fruits, and the outer dark leaves of savoy cabbage contain much more carotene than the inner pale ones. During digestion this carotene is converted into Vitamin A.

In all methods of cooking savoury foods, the vegetables must always be washed, drained and patted dry, and if necessary peeled with a potato peeler. Slicing, dicing and chopping must be done neatly in geometrical shapes. The blanching of most vegetables is done to eliminate bitter juices. Salting courgettes (zucchini), aubergines (eggplants) and cucumber for 30 minutes before using them achieves the same result. Certain vegetables, such as potatoes and artichokes, will change colour if not soaked in cold water with vinegar or lemon slices, before cooking. Dry vegetables will always benefit from being soaked in distilled or spring water. Hard water tends to coat them with insoluble minerals. Pulses will take less time to cook if they are soaked for at least one hour. Beans and chick peas must be soaked overnight and will take 2 hours to cook in the oven, kept covered with a lid.

Braised Chicory

The French and Americans call chicory *endive*, but in England the white chicons are referred to as Belgian chicory. Gourmets like the bitterness of this vegetable which can be eaten raw in salads. Cooked in lemon juice and butter it is very popular as a garnish for veal or pork escalopes. To reduce the bitterness, cut a cone-shaped core out of the base of each head.

―――――――――― ∾ SERVES 4 ∾ ――――――――――

8 heads of white leaf chicory
100 ml (3½ fl oz · 6½ tbsp) chicken or veal stock or water
100 g (4 oz · ½ cup) butter
Juice of 1 lemon
Salt and freshly ground black pepper
Pinch of sugar
30 ml (2 tbsp) chopped parsley

1. Place the chicory in a casserole dish (Dutch oven). Cover with the stock or water, butter and lemon juice. Season to taste and add the sugar. Cover and simmer gently on top of the oven for 45 minutes.

Sprinkle with parsley before serving.

Preparation time: 5 minutes.
Cooking time: 45 minutes.

Milanese-style Courgettes

Marrow (squash) and courgettes (zucchini) have a mild flavour, but being very watery they can be cooked in their own juice. This Milanese recipe is probably the best way to add extra flavour.

─────────────── ∽ SERVES 4 ∾ ───────────────

4 courgettes (zucchini), sliced slantwise
4 small tomatoes, skinned, seeded and chopped
2 garlic cloves, chopped
4 mushrooms, sliced
1 shallot, chopped
Salt and freshly ground black pepper
5 ml (1 tsp) celery seed
Pinch of saffron or pinch of curry powder
60 ml (4 tbsp) olive oil
Parmesan cheese, grated

1. Place all ingredients, except the cheese, in a casserole. Cover tightly with a lid. Cook for 20 minutes at 180°C/350°F/gas mark 4.

Serve with grated Parmesan cheese handed separately.

Preparation time: 10 minutes.
Cooking time: 20 minutes.

Field Mushroom and Herb Casserole

Casseroled mushrooms have a better flavour than if fried or grilled. This particular dish, with chopped ham and a mixture of herbs, has become popular in many regions of France. It can also be eaton on fried bread or toast.

─── ∽ SERVES 4 ∾ ───

450 g (1 lb) field mushrooms
or a mixture of wild cap mushrooms, giroles, ceps, etc.)
45 ml (3 tbsp) olive oil
3 garlic cloves, chopped
100 g (4 oz · 1 cup) ham with a little fat, diced
1 shallot, chopped
30 ml (2 tbsp) chopped mixed herbs
(parsley, chives, basil, tarragon)
120 ml (4 fl oz · ½ cup) medium sherry

1. Trim the stalks off the mushrooms. Peel and quarter the caps. Wash, drain and pat dry in a clean cloth or kitchen paper.

2. Place all the ingredients in a casserole (Dutch oven). Cover and braise in a hot oven for 10 minutes at 200°C/400°F/gas mark 6.

Preparation time: 15 minutes.
Cooking time: 10 minutes.

Italian-style Fennel

This delicious aniseed-scented bulb is very underrated in Britain. Yet, like celery, it can be one of the most flavoursome garnishes or basis for a main dish for vegetarians.

───────────── ∾ SERVES 4 ∾ ─────────────

4 fennel bulbs
300 ml (½ pt · 1¼ cups) water
45 ml (3 tbsp) olive oil
1 tomato, skinned, seeded and chopped

Garnish:
100 g (4 oz · 1 cup) Parmesan cheese, grated
30 ml (2 tbsp) chopped parsley
2 hard-boiled (hard-cooked) eggs, chopped (optional)

1. Trim away the upper stems, leaving just the bulbous roots of the fennel. Set the fine, feathery leaves aside. Trim the root base, cut each fennel in half lengthways, and rinse under cold water.

2. Place the fennel in a casserole (Dutch oven) with the water or stock and the oil. Season to taste. Cover with the chopped tomato. Cover and braise for 45 minutes at 180°C/350°F/gas mark 4.

On serving, sprinkle over the Parmesan, parsley and chopped eggs (if using).

Preparation time: 10 minutes.
Cooking time: 45 minutes.

Long-grain Rice Casserole

High quality American rice can be cooked in 20 minutes complete with an assortment of flavoured ingredients. This recipe is central to the vegetarian diet.

———————————— ∾ SERVES 4 ∾ ————————————

150 g (5 oz · ⅔ cup) long-grain rice
1 onion, chopped
2 garlic cloves, chopped
5 ml (1 tsp) saffron or turmeric
100 g (4 oz · 1 cup) peas
1 sweet red (bell) pepper, seeded and diced
600 ml (1 pt · 2½ cups) chicken stock
50 g (2 oz · ¼ cup) butter
Salt and freshly ground black pepper

1. Combine all ingredients in a casserole (Dutch oven). Cover and braise for 20–25 minutes at 200°C/400°F/gas mark 6. This rapid cooking method will help the liquid to evaporate and leave the rice grains separated.
2. After 10 minutes stir the mixture with a fork.

Preparation time: 10 minutes.
Cooking time: 20–25 minutes.

So far, I have grouped together vegetable recipes which answer the description of casserole cookery. For nutritional purposes I have also made a point of using recipes which contain protein. But the stews and vegetable casseroles can also be enriched with eggs, nuts, fish, meat and poultry or cooked with meaty flavours. The best way to obtain good flavour development in a casserole is to start by frying (sautéing) the onions, garlic and root vegetables before adding the pulses or pre-cooked beans and starchy vegetables. These only take 20 minutes to cook (like rice or potatoes). Leafy vegetables, herbs and spices may be added at the last minute.

In this section I have included an old hot pot potato stew my grandmother used to cook every day of her life (although it included a very small piece of beef flank or knuckle of bacon for my grandfather. She was a gardener and grew and cooked her own vegetables all her life. Hot pot cookery is not just hash and minced meat or overcooked cabbage stew, but well balanced meals in their own right. A change from boiled carrots, boiled sprouts or boiled potatoes!

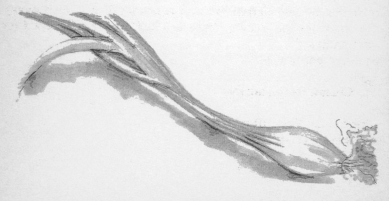

Aubergine Casserole

Often known as eggplant because of its smooth egg shape, the aubergine is now grown successfully in Britain in greenhouses. The best are imported from Spain, Italy, the South of France and from Middle Eastern countries. The flavour is in the skin and for this reason the aubergine will taste better with the skin on. To eliminate the bitter taste you can either sprinkle salt over the cut pieces or soak in running water.

∽ SERVES 4 ∾

2 aubergines (eggplants), cut into thick cubes of 2.5 cm (1 in)
2 courgettes (zucchini), cut into thick cubes of 2.5 cm (1 in)
2 tomatoes, skinned, seeded and diced
1 large onion, sliced
45 ml (3 tbsp) olive oil
3 basil leaves, chopped
Salt and freshly ground black pepper
300 ml (½ pt · 1¼ cups) water
5 ml (1 tsp) sugar

Garnish:
100 g (4 oz · 1 cup) roasted peanuts

1. Soak the cut aubergines and courgettes for 5 minutes in cold running water. Drain well.

2. Put all the ingredients in a casserole dish (Dutch oven). Season to taste and cover. Braise at 180°C/350°F/gas mark 4 for 45 minutes.

Serve hot or cold.

 Chianti to accompany.

Preparation time: 10 minutes.
Cooking time: 45 minutes.

Broad Bean Casserole in Buttermilk

Mature broad (lima) beans should be shelled, par-boiled for 6 minutes, and the tough skin of each seed removed, leaving the tender green flesh. When prepared in this way this vegetable is delicious in soured cream and flaked almonds.

───────────── ∽ SERVES 4 ∼ ─────────────

450 g (1 lb · 4 cups) broad (lima) beans, shelled, boiled and skinned
120 ml (4 fl oz · ½ cup) buttermilk
Salt and freshly ground black pepper
1 shallot, chopped
100 g (4 oz · 1 cup) flaked almonds

1. In a shallow casserole (Dutch oven) place the par-boiled, skinned broad beans, buttermilk, shallots and almonds. Cover and cook for 20 minutes at 200°C/400°F/gas mark 6. Season before serving.

Preparation time: 10 minutes.
Cooking time: 20 minutes.

Breton Haricot Bean Casserole

This variety of haricot beans are also known as navy or Michigan beans. They require soaking in distilled water for 6 hours. If you use hard water the insoluble minerals will cling to the beans and make them tough. If you use soda water to tenderise them they will crack open. By using distilled water you avoid all these problems. Similarly, you can use red, black, green, flageolet, lima or butterbeans in the same way.

────────────── ∽ SERVES 4 ∽ ──────────────

450 g (1 lb · 4 cups) haricot (navy) beans,
soaked in distilled water for 6 hours
1 carrot, diced
1 onion, chopped
2 large tomatoes, skinned, seeded and chopped
2 garlic cloves, chopped
5 ml (1 tsp) freshly ground black pepper
(no salt needed until the beans are cooked)
Sprig of thyme
30 ml (2 tbsp) olive oil
1 l (1¾ pts · 4¼ cups) water

1. Put all the ingredients in a casserole (Dutch oven). Cover and cook slowly for 2 hours at 180°C/350°F/gas mark 4. Season when cooked.

Preparation time: 10 minutes plus soaking time.
Cooking time: 2 hours.

Carrot and Parsnip Casserole

This is a dish which improves with slow cooking. The natural sugar in the root vegetables plus the honey and butter combine to give this dish its unique flavour and fragrance.

―――――――――――――― ∽ SERVES 4 ∽ ――――――――――――――

450 g (1 lb · 4 cups) carrots, cut slantwise
450 g (1 lb · 4 cups) parsnips, cut in sticks, then sliced
30 ml (2 tbsp) clear honey
75 g (3 oz · 1/3 cup) butter
1 onion, chopped
300 ml (1/2 pt · 1 1/4 cups) water
3 mint leaves, chopped

1. Place all the ingredients in a casserole (Dutch oven). Cover with a lid and cook on low heat at 180°C/350°F/gas mark 4 for 1 hour until the liquid is almost evaporated. Season to taste.

Preparation time: 10 minutes.
Cooking time: 1 hour.

Nepal-style Cauliflower

Cauliflower is often bland and overcooked. To prevent this soak the cauliflower in an acid such as vinegar or lemon juice. The finished dish should be crisp and not mushy. Before cooking, cut off the outer leaves and the main core. There is no need to remove the inner tender green leaves. In this casserole dish the vegetable retains its flavour and crispness.

───────────────── ∽ SERVES 4 ∾ ─────────────────

1 cauliflower
Juice and grated rind of 1 lemon
300 ml (½ pt · 1¼ cups) water
Salt and freshly ground black pepper
5 ml (1 tsp) made mild mustard
5 ml (1 tsp) clear honey
5 ml (1 tsp) saffron or Madras curry powder
120 ml (4 fl oz · ½ cup) yoghurt
30 ml (2 tbsp) chopped coriander (cilantro) leaves

1. Divide the cauliflower into florets. Soak them in the lemon juice and grated rind. Place in a casserole (Dutch oven). Cover with water and season to taste.
2. Cook, uncovered, in a moderate oven for 30 minutes at 180°C/350°F/gas mark 4.
3. Mix the mustard, honey, saffron or Madras curry powder and yoghurt and blend into the cauliflower liquid when the dish is ready. Sprinkle the coriander over the cauliflower sprigs and serve.

Preparation time: 15 minutes.
Cooking time: 30 minutes.

Braised Celery Casserole

Small heads of celery are used for this casserole. They should be cut 8 cm (3 in) long and cut in half, including some of the root (the celery heads). This French recipe is often served with roast pheasant, guinea fowl, or on its own.

―――――――――――― ∽ SERVES 4 ∽ ――――――――――――

2 heads of celery
25 g (1 oz · 2 tbsp) butter
600 ml (1 pt · 2½ cups) chicken or veal stock
Salt and freshly ground black pepper

Garnish:
150 g (5 oz · 1¼ cups) Cheddar cheese, grated
30 ml (2 tbsp) chopped parsley

1. Trim the root off each head of celery. Wash and scrub under cold running water. Par-boil them for 10 minutes in water in a shallow casserole (Dutch oven). Drain and cut each head in half.

2. Melt the butter in the bottom of the casserole. Arrange the celery on top and cover with the stock. Season to taste. Braise for 1 hour at 180°C/350°F/gas mark 4 with the lid on.

Sprinkle over the grated cheese and parsley and serve with a trickle of the reduced stock.

Preparation time: 15 minutes.
Cooking time: 1 hour.

Mexican Sweetcorn Casserole with Chilli

Sweetcorn is also known as maize or Indian corn. The kernels can be cooked in a casserole with diced red (bell) peppers and chilli as a tasty and nourishing dish often enriched with baked beans or peas for protein. With more stock this could be served as *Pancho Villa* soup.

―――――――――――――― ∾ SERVES 4 ∾ ――――――――――――――

450 g (1 lb · 4 cups) sweetcorn (corn) kernels
1 red (bell) pepper, seeded and diced
1 onion, chopped
150 g (5 oz · 1¼ cups) peas
1 green chilli, deseeded and chopped
600 ml (1 pt · 2½ cups) water or chicken stock
Salt and freshly ground black pepper

Garnish:
1 avocado, peeled and diced at the last moment
100 ml (3½ fl oz · 6½ tbsp) single (light) cream

1. Place all the ingredients, except the garnish, in a casserole (Dutch oven). Cover and braise for 1 hour at 180°C/350°F/gas mark 4. Drain away some of the surplus cooking liquid.

2. Mix in the cream and diced avocado. Check and adjust the seasoning before serving.

Preparation time: 10 minutes.
Cooking time: 1 hour.

Indian-style Potato Casserole

This is one of my favourite potato dishes. In combination with cabbage, the potatoes, flavoured with strong curry powder, make a meal on their own. Use new potatoes or the red-skinned waxy kind which do not break up.

——————————— ∾ SERVES 4 ∾ ———————————

450 g (1 lb) new potatoes, scrubbed
1 onion, chopped
60 ml (4 tbsp) oil
15 ml (1 tbsp) curry powder
15 ml (1 tbsp) tomato purée (paste)
150 g (5 oz · 1¼ cups) white cabbage shredded or chopped
600 ml (1 pt · 2½ cups) water
1 garlic clove, chopped
100 g (4 oz · 1 cup) peas
Salt and freshly ground black pepper
30 ml (2 tbsp) desiccated (shredded) coconut, toasted

1. Place all the ingredients together in a casserole (Dutch oven). Cover and braise in the oven for 45 minutes at 180°C/ 350°F/gas mark 4.
2. Sprinkle slightly toasted desiccated coconut over the potatoes. Drain away some of the juice or use it as gravy.

Preparation time: 10 minutes.
Cooking time: 45 minutes.

Chick Pea Casserole

Chick peas (garbanzos) take 2 hours to cook even after being soaked overnight in distilled water. However, they are now available in cans. Despite their name, they are no relation to the pea family. They have a high protein content (like soya beans).

----------------- ∾ SERVES 4 ∾ -----------------

150 g (5 oz · scant 1 cup) chick peas (garbanzos), soaked overnight
600 ml (1 pt · 2½ cups) water
1 onion, chopped
45 ml (3 tbsp) sesame oil
Pinch of ground cumin
Salt and freshly ground black pepper
150 g (5 oz · 1¼ cups) spinach, shredded

1. Put all the ingredients in a casserole (Dutch oven) and cover. Simmer gently for 2 hours. Check after 1 hour to make sure there is enough liquid and add more water if needed.

Preparation time: 5 minutes plus soaking.
Cooking time: 2 hours.

Latin American Gombo Casserole

'Ladies' fingers', or okra, as this pod is called, is now available in most supermarkets. It is a nutritious and very gelatinous vegetable and is one of the most popular ingredients in Indian cookery.

―――――――――― ∽ SERVES 4 ∽ ――――――――――

450 g (1 lb) okra
45 ml (3 tbsp) oil
1 onion, chopped
3 tomatoes, skinned, seeded and chopped
3 garlic cloves, chopped
15 ml (1 tbsp) curry powder
1 green chilli, seeded and chopped
Salt to taste
300 ml (½ pt · 1¼ cups) water

Garnish:
100 g (4 oz · 1 cup) grated hard cheese or chopped peanuts

1. Remove the stalks from the okra without bursting the pods.
2. Place all the ingredients in a casserole dish (Dutch oven). Cover and braise in oven for 30 minutes at 200°C/400°F/gas mark 6. Season with salt and sprinkle over the cheese or peanuts on serving.

Preparation time: 10 minutes.
Cooking time: 30 minutes.

Sauerkraut and Frankfurter Casserole

All over central Europe and in most parts of Russia, fermented cabbage (called sauerkraut) is served as a main vegetable braised with ham or bacon and with Frankfurters. In Britain it is not so common and can only be obtained in cans. If it is not available use Savoy cabbage, as in this recipe.

───────────── ∽ SERVES 4 ∽ ─────────────

1 savoy cabbage, shredded
(or canned sauerkraut, rinsed and drained)
1 small apple, grated
50 g (2 oz · ¼ cup) butter
6 juniper berries (gin berries)
6 crushed peppercorns
1 onion, chopped
5 ml (1 tsp) salt
4 Frankfurters
4 thick slices of garlic sausage
8 new potatoes, scrubbed and sliced
15 ml (1 tbsp) olive oil
300 ml (½ pt · 1¼ cups) water
300 ml (½ pt · 1¼ cups) dry white wine

1. In a casserole (Dutch oven) place all the ingredients in layers, sprinkle over the oil and add the water and wine. Cover and braise for 45 minutes to 1 hour at 180°C/350°F/gas mark 4.

Preparation time: 10 minutes.
Cooking time: 45 minutes–1 hour.

Welsh-style Leek Casserole

Young leeks are best for this casserole so that both the white and green parts can be used. To remove any dirt embedded in the leek, insert the point of the knife in the middle of each one and cut from the middle towards the green part in a zig-zag pattern. This operation will open up the leek so that the dirt will be removed when the leek is washed under cold running water.

───────────── ∽ SERVES 4 ∽ ─────────────

8 small leeks, trimmed and cleaned
4 slices of ham
300 ml (½ pt · 1¼ cups) chicken stock
100 ml (3½ fl oz · 6½ tbsp) dry sherry
Salt and freshly ground black pepper
100 g (4 oz · 1 cup) Welsh hard cheese, grated

1. Place the leeks and ham in layers in a casserole (Dutch oven). Cover with the stock and sherry. Season to taste and cover. Braise for 35 minutes at 200°C/400°F/gas mark 6.

Drain off the surplus liquid and sprinkle over grated cheese before serving.

Preparation time: 5 minutes.
Cooking time: 35 minutes.

Casserole of Pumpkin with Peanuts

Pumpkin is better known as a dessert ingredient, but in many countries it is cooked like marrow and enjoyed for its distinctive flavour.

∼ SERVES 4 ∽

450 g (1 lb · 4 cups) pumpkin, peeled, seeded and cut into cubes
1 onion, chopped
1 piece of root ginger (ginger root), peeled and chopped
4 rashers (slices) bacon, rinded and diced
600 ml (1 pt · 2½ cups) water or chicken stock
50 g (2 oz · ¼ cup) butter
Salt and freshly ground black pepper

1. In a casserole (Dutch oven) combine all the ingredients. Cover and cook for 30 minutes at 200°C/400°F/gas mark 6. Drain off the surplus liquid and serve on its own.

Preparation time: 15 minutes.
Cooking time: 30 minutes.

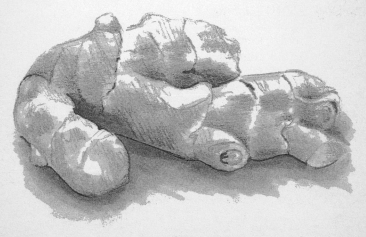

Sweet and Sour Casseroled Onions with Sultanas

This dish is more of a garnish or starter, yet it is cooked like a casserole to concentrate the flavour. Select onions weighing 50 g (2 oz) maximum. Uniformity is important for presentation.

───────────── ∾ SERVES 4 ∾ ─────────────

16 onions, peeled neatly
50 ml (2 fl oz · 3½ tbsp) wine vinegar
50 g (2 oz) clear honey
50 g (2 oz · ¼ cup) sugar
100 ml (3½ fl oz · 6½ tbsp) sweet white wine
5 ml (1 tsp) anise seeds
50 g (2 oz · ⅓ cup) sultanas (golden raisins)
100 ml (3½ fl oz · 6½ tbsp) water
Salt and freshly ground black pepper

1. Place the ingredients in a shallow casserole (Dutch oven). Cover and braise for 45 minutes at 180°C/350°F/gas mark 4 until the liquid has evaporated. Check every 10 minutes. If necessary, cook for a little longer to reduce the liquid.

2. Serve cold as an *hors d'oeuvre* or as an accompaniment for cold meat.

Preparation time: 15 minutes.
Cooking time: 45 minutes.

French-style Petits Pois

There was a time when peas were a novelty enjoyed only by the rich. This dish was famous at the time of Louis XIV, but has never caught on in Britain because the peas do not look green after being cooked in a casserole. The dish is well worth trying because the peas taste better and sweeter than plainly boiled with mint in the English style.

~ SERVES 4 ~

1 lettuce heart, shredded
450 g (1 lb · 4 cups) shelled fresh peas
12 button (pearl) onions, no bigger than grapes, peeled
100 g (4 oz · ½ cup) butter
120 ml (4 fl oz · ½ cup) water
Salt and freshly ground black pepper
5 ml (1 tsp) sugar
5 ml (1 tsp) cornflour (cornstarch)

1. Place all ingredients in an earthenware casserole (Dutch oven). Cover and braise for 30 minutes at 180°C/350°F/gas mark 4. Blend the cornflour with 10 ml (2 tsp) water. Stir into the casserole. Bring to the boil, stirring and simmer for 1 minute.

This dish can be served either on its own or with duck.

Preparation time: 10 minutes.
Cooking time: 30 minutes.

Green Lentils with Hazelnuts

This nourishing dish can be served alone or as a substitute for meat.

───────────── ∼ SERVES 4 ∼ ─────────────

150 g (5 oz · scant 1 cup) green lentils, soaked for 2 hours
150 g (5 oz · 1¼ cups) hazelnuts
150 g (5 oz · 1¼ cups) small onions, peeled
2 tomatoes, skinned, seeded and chopped
15 ml (1 tbsp) yeast extract
600 ml (1 pt · 2½ cups) water
Salt and freshly ground black pepper
50 g (2 oz · ¼ cup) butter

1. Place all the ingredients in a casserole dish (Dutch oven) and braise for 40 minutes at 180°C/350°F/gas mark 4. Pour away any excess liquid.

This dish can be eaten cold with a French dressing or hot mixed with cooked rice.

Preparation time: 10 minutes plus soaking time.
Cooking time: 40 minutes.

FRUIT CASSEROLES

THERE ARE MANY TYPES OF FRESH AND dried fruits which gain in flavour from being poached in a syrup casserole-style. The addition of spices such as cinnamon, cloves, aniseed, mint and lemon grass, or citrus peel gives a special fragrance. The fragile texture of many fruits requires slow cooking to allow the syrup to permeate the flesh of the fruit, while preventing the skin from splitting and the flesh from disintegrating.

In this chapter I have selected 10 fruits which make ideal compôtes. The compôtes can also be served with ice cream or with set custards, or alone (preferably cold).

With certain syrups, I recommend that a tea bag be added towards the end of the cooking time to give a tang to the syrup.

Oriental Fig Casserole

There are over 600 species of fig grown in the world. The white, pink and black figs are the three main varieties of which the Bourgassote, Aubique, Blanquette, purple Dauphine and the Greek figs are the best-known types. Fig syrup is an excellent laxative and recommended as a good source of fibre on account of its pin-sized seeds. Figs are the sweetest fruit on earth and for this reason there is no need to add as much sugar as for other fruits.

―――――― ∾ SERVES 4 ∾ ――――――

1 kg (2¼ lb) fresh red figs
150 g (5 oz · ⅔ cup) fresh raspberries
150 g (5 oz · ⅔ cup) sugar
1 cinnamon stick
4 lemon slices
150 ml (¼ pt · ⅔ cup) red wine
300 ml (½ pt · 1¼ cups) water

1. Wash and pat dry the figs. Place in a casserole (Dutch oven) with the other ingredients and cook for 30 minutes at 180°C/350°F/gas mark 4. Serve with rice or semolina (cream of wheat) pudding and almond biscuits (cookies).

Preparation time: 5 minutes.
Cooking time: 30 minutes.

Pear Compôte

Pears, which are native to Europe and Western Asia, have been cultivated since earliest times. Six hundred varieties are available in the world although all the best-known varieties are dessert fruits. Pears are usually cooked when they are still firm and not completely ripe. For flavour, it is best to use ripe pears with the peel added as a separate flavour enhancer. William, Conference or Doyenne de Comice are the best varieties.

------- ∾ SERVES 4 ∾ -------

4 Comice pears
5 ml (1 tsp) aniseed seeds or 15 ml (1 tbsp) Anisette liqueur
300 ml (½ pt · 1¼ cups) water
150 g (5 oz · ⅔ cup) sugar
4 cloves
1 tea bag

1. Peel the pears then cut them in half and remove the cores. Place the peel and seeds (if using) in a casserole (Dutch oven) with the water, sugar and cloves.

2. Arrange the pears on top of the other ingredients. Gently simmer, covered, for 30 minutes.

3. Remove the casserole and add the tea bag. Leave for 8 minutes and then remove. Strain the syrup and serve it with the pears. At the last minute sprinkle over a little anisette liqueur if the anis seeds have not been used.

Preparation time: 10 minutes.
Cooking time: 30 minutes plus standing time.

Peaches and Nectarines in Blackcurrant Cordial

Peaches should be peeled for cooked desserts, but not nectarines. To make the peeling of peaches easier, scald them in boiling water for 1–2 minutes then immerse them in cold water. Peel the skins downwards in strips, using a small knife. Cut the peaches in half and remove the stones. Leave the nectarines whole.

―――――――――――――― ∾ SERVES 4 ∾ ――――――――――――――

4 peaches
4 nectarines
30 ml (2 tbsp) blackcurrant cordial
150 g (5 oz · ⅔ cup) granulated sugar
300 ml (½ pt · 1¼ cups) water
45 ml (3 tbsp) brandy or gin

1. Put the peaches (peeled, halved and stoned (pitted)) in a casserole (Dutch oven) with the nectarines. Add the blackcurrant cordial, sugar and water. Poach in the oven at 180°C/350°F/gas mark 4 for 15 minutes. Cool in the syrup and serve with ice cream. Add brandy or gin before serving.

Preparation time: 5 minutes.
Cooking time: 15 minutes.

Apple Casserole

Dessert apples are best used for compôtes as they do not disintegrate on cooking. The best varieties for this kind of sweet are Cox's Orange Pippin, Orleans Reinette and Egremont Russet.

────────────── ∽ SERVES 4 ∾ ──────────────

8 eating (dessert) apples, cored and peeled
300 ml (½ pt · 1¼ cups) apple juice
50 g (5 oz · ⅔ cup) brown sugar
Juice of 1 lemon
1 cinnamon stick

1. Place all the ingredients in a casserole dish (Dutch oven). Cover and cook gently for 20 minutes at 180°C/350°F/gas mark 4. Cool and serve with soured (dairy sour) cream or yoghurt.

Preparation time: 5 minutes.
Cooking time: 20 minutes.

Apricot Casserole in Lime Cordial

Apricots can be cooked in just 6 minutes. If overheated they tend to get mushy. This delicate fruit is enhanced with Kirsch. This is my favourite method of cooking them.

~ SERVES 4 ~
---

1 kg (2¼ lb) fresh apricots, firm and not too ripe
300 ml (½ pt · 1¼ cups) freshly brewed Ceylon tea
100 ml (3½ fl oz · 6½ tbsp) lime cordial
100 g (4 oz · ½ cup) granulated sugar
30 ml (2 tbsp) Kirsch (optional)

1. Wipe the apricots gently with a damp cloth as they bruise easily. They can be cut into halves and the stones (pits) removed, although they are best left whole.

2. Brew the tea and strain it into the casserole dish (Dutch oven). Add the apricots, lime cordial and sugar. Cover with a lid and poach for 6 minutes at 180°C/350°F/gas mark 4. Cool in the syrup and add the Kirsch before serving.

This compôte is ideal with cream, ice cream or rice pudding.

Preparation time: 10 minutes.
Cooking time: 6 minutes plus cooling.

Prunes in Red Wine

Californian stoned prunes are best for this kind of dessert.

1 kg (1¾ lb) Californian prunes, stoned (pitted)
300 ml (½ pt · 1¼ cups) red wine
5 ml (1 tsp) ground cinnamon
Pinch of ground nutmeg and cloves
4 slices of lemon

1. Soak the prunes in the wine with the spices and lemon for 3 hours until swollen. Place in a casserole dish (Dutch oven) and cook gently at 180°C/350°F/gas mark 4 for 20 minutes. Remove the lemon.

Cool and serve with rice pudding, blancmange or shortbread (shortcake).

Preparation time: 2 minutes plus soaking time.
Cooking time: 20 minutes plus cooling.

Fruit Compôte Casserole

In the winter, a mixture of dried fruits can be enjoyed in a compôte consisting of apples, prunes, pears, raisins, apricots and peaches. To maximise the flavour, these fruits should be soaked in freshly brewed tea until swollen.

～ SERVES 4 ～

450 g (1 lb) assorted dried fruits
600 ml (1 pt · 2½ cups) freshly brewed tea, strained
50 g (2 oz) clear honey
100 g (4 oz · ½ cup) brown sugar
5 ml (1 tsp) ground cinnamon
Juice of 1 lemon

1. Place the fruit in a casserole (Dutch oven). Pour in the strained tea. Soak for 3 hours then stir in the honey and cinnamon. Cook in the oven at 180°C/350°F/gas mark 4 for 30 minutes. Cool and chill overnight. Add the lemon juice before serving with ice cream or hot custard.

Preparation time: 5 minutes plus soaking time.
Cooking time: 30 minutes plus cooling and chilling time.

Stewed Gooseberries

Sweet red or yellow gooseberries are usually served fresh as a dessert fruit. The smaller and harder acid gooseberries are only suitable for cooking. Cooked gooseberries can be used as fillings for pies and puddings, and creamed desserts such as fools, as well as for sauces for grilled mackerel or pork.

───────────── ∾ SERVES 4 ∾ ─────────────

10 ml (2 tsp) cornflour (cornstarch)
300 ml (½ pt · 1¼ cups) boiling water
150 ml (¼ pt · ⅔ cup) white wine
1 kg (2¼ lb) green gooseberries
150 g (5 oz · ⅔ cup) granulated sugar
1 piece of root ginger (ginger root), chopped

1. Prepare a slightly thickened syrup by blending the cornflour with 45 ml (3 tbsp) of cold water in a casserole dish (Dutch oven). Add the boiling water. Cook for 4 minutes to clear the starch. Add the white wine and boil for 2 more minutes.

2. Prepare the gooseberries by snipping off the flower and stalk ('topping and tailing') with scissors. Wash them carefully and drain them in a colander.

3. Place the fruit in the casserole. Add the sugar and ginger. Poach for 6 minutes at 180°C/350°F/gas mark 4 or until slightly soft. Cool in the sauce and serve with custard.

Preparation time: 20 minutes.
Cooking time: 6 minutes.

Rhubarb and Strawberry Compôte

There can be no better combination for flavour and refreshing taste than tender, pink rhubarb. Forced for use in late winter and early spring it has a more delicate, less acid, flavour than the thicker and coarser main crop stalks of June and July. In combination with other fruits, such as strawberries, it acquires added dimensions of flavour and colour. The addition of ginger, too, can make a big difference. Main crop rhubarb is very fibrous and has to be scraped well all over. The best way to cook it to prevent pulping is in a casserole (Dutch oven) with a heavy syrup which will hold the fruit together firmly.

———————————— ∾ SERVES 4 ∾ ————————————

450 g (1 lb) fresh rhubarb, scraped if maincrop and
cut in pieces 3 cm (1¼ in) long
150 g (5 oz · ⅔ cup) fresh strawberries
1 small piece of root ginger (ginger root), grated
150 ml (¼ pt · ½ cup) red or rosé wine
225 g (½ lb · 1 cup) granulated sugar
25 g (1 oz · 2 tbsp) powdered gelatine
2 drops of red colouring

1. Place the fruit in a casserole (Dutch oven) with the ginger and wine.
2. Mix the sugar and gelatine, colour with two drops of red colouring, and sprinkle this mixture over the fruits. Cover with a lid and cook for 8 minutes at 180°C/350°F/gas mark 4. Cool and chill.

Serve with custard or ice cream.

Preparation time: 10 minutes.
Cooking time: 8 minutes.

Jamaican Butterscotch Bananas

Bananas have their best flavour when they are eaten either very ripe or baked in a casserole. My favourite way cooks them with butter, sugar and rum and is a recipe I brought back from my stay in Jamaica.

───────────── ∾ SERVES 4 ∾ ─────────────

8 bananas, not too ripe
100 g (4 oz · ½ cup) caster (superfine) sugar
100 g (4 oz · ½ cup) unsalted butter
Juice of 1 orange
15 ml (1 tbsp) Jamaican rum

1. Peel the bananas and place them in a casserole (Dutch oven) with the sugar, butter and orange juice. Bake for 10 minutes at 180°C/350°F/gas mark 4 until the butter turns into a creamy and sticky butterscotch. Remove and cool.

Serve with chocolate or coffee ice cream.

Preparation time: 5 minutes.
Cooking time: 10 minutes.

Index